THE NORTON LIBRARY

Lysistrata

AARON POOCHIGIAN earned a PhD in Classics from the University of Minnesota and an MFA in poetry from Columbia University. He is the translator of, among other classical works, Sappho's poetry (published under the title *Stung with Love*), Apollonius's *Jason and the Argonauts*, and four plays by Aristophanes: *Lysistrata*, *Clouds*, *Birds*, and *Women of the Assembly*. He has published two books of poetry—*The Cosmic Purr* and *Manhattanite*—and a novel-in-verse, *Mr. Either/Or*. His poems have appeared in such publications as *Best American Poetry*, the *Paris Review*, and *POETRY*.

THE NORTON LIBRARY

2021–2022

Euripides, Medea
  Translated by Sheila Murnaghan

Sophocles, Oedipus Tyrannos
  Translated by Emily Wilson

Aristophanes, Lysistrata
  Translated by Aaron Poochigian

Murasaki, The Tale of Genji
  Translated and Abridged by Dennis Washburn

Locke, Second Treatise of Government
  Edited by A. John Simmons

Rousseau, Discourse on the Origin of Inequality
  Translated by Julia Conaway Bondanella and Edited by Frederick Neuhouser

Shelley, Frankenstein
  Edited by Michael Bérubé

Mill, Utilitarianism
  Edited by Katarzyna de Lazari-Radek and Peter Singer

Dostoevsky, Notes from Underground
  Translated by Michael R. Katz

Woolf, Mrs. Dalloway
  Edited by Merve Emre

For a complete list of titles in the Norton Library, visit
wwnorton.com/norton-library

THE NORTON LIBRARY

Aristophanes
Lysistrata

Translated by

Aaron Poochigian

W. W. NORTON & COMPANY
Independent Publishers Since 1923

Copyright © 2021 by Aaron Poochigian
Previously published in *ARISTOPHANES: FOUR PLAYS*: Clouds, Birds, Lysistrata, Women of the Assembly

All rights reserved
Printed in the United States of America
First Edition

Editor: Pete Simon
Associate Editor: Katie Pak
Project Editor: Maura Gaughan
Manufacturing by LSC Communications
Compositor: Westchester Publishing Services
Book design by Marisa Nakasone
Production manager: Jeremy Burton

Library of Congress Cataloging-in-Publication Data

Names: Aristophanes, author. | Poochigian, Aaron, 1973– translator.
Title: Lysistrata / Aristophanes ; translated by Aaron Poochigian.
Other titles: Lysistrata. English (Poochigian) | Norton library.
Description: First edition. | New York : W. W. Norton & Company, 2021. |
    Series: The Norton library | Includes bibliographical references.
Identifiers: LCCN 2020055793 | **ISBN 9780393870831 (paperback)** | ISBN
    9780393885293 (epub)
Subjects: LCSH: Lysistrata (Fictitious character)—Drama. | Women—Greece—
    Athens--Drama. | Peace movements—Greece—Athens—Drama. | Women
    and peace—Greece—Athens—Drama. | Man-woman relationships—Greece—
    Athens—Drama. | Greece—History—Peloponnesian War, 4314–04—Drama |
    LCGFT: Drama. | Comedy plays.
Classification: LCC PA3877 .L8 2021 | DDC 882/.01—dc23
LC record available at https://lccn.loc.gov/2020055793

ISBN: 978-0-393-87083-1 (pbk.)

W. W. Norton & Company, Inc., 500 Fifth Avenue, New York, N.Y. 10110
www.wwnorton.com

W. W. Norton & Company Ltd., 15 Carlisle Street, London W1D 3BS

1 2 3 4 5 6 7 8 9 0

Contents

vii   Introduction

xviii   A Note on the Translation

1   LYSISTRATA

86   Notes

Introduction

Apart from evidence in his comedies themselves, we know next to nothing about Aristophanes. An anonymous *Life* informs us that he was the son of one Philippus and belonged to the deme (district) Cydathenaeum, in Athens, which included the Acropolis, but we do not know, for example, whether his family was rich or poor. Lines in his play *Peace* (421 B.C.E.) inform us that he went bald at a young age, but we know nothing more of his appearance. Even the dates of his birth and death are unclear (though circa 446–386 B.C.E. is the general consensus).

We learn more about Aristophanes from his plays' *parabases*. Common in fifth-century B.C.E. comedy, these interludes, in which the actors exit and leave the chorus alone onstage, are occasionally employed by Aristophanes to speak directly to the audience. From them we learn details about his early and middle years. A *parabasis* in the play *Clouds* reveals that he was a precocious playwright, having had his first two plays, *Banqueters* (427 B.C.E.) and *Babylonians* (426 B.C.E.), produced for him because he had not yet reached an age at which he could produce them himself. This precociousness wasn't just a matter of artistic talent; he was also preternaturally drawn to controversy from the very start of his career. In *Babylonians*, before he was even twenty, Aristophanes initiated a vehement campaign of ridicule against the famous general and demagogue Cleon, who rose to political prominence by opposing the more cautious strategy of the preeminent statesman Pericles (ca. 495–429 B.C.E.) in the Peloponnesian War. Mockery of prominent citizens (who were likely in the audience) is a hallmark of Aristophanic comedy, but Aristophanes's insults targeting Cleon are especially virulent. After his initial attack, Cleon, in revenge, prosecuted him for "wronging the city," but the young man was acquitted. In his next play, Acharnians (425 B.C.E.), Aristophanes threatens, through the chorus, to "cut [Cleon] up to make soles for the Horsemen's shoes" (lines 299–302), and this threat is fulfilled in *The Knights* (424 B.C.E.), in which he again attacks Cleon, portraying him, onstage, as a deceitful and corrupt warmonger. Subsequently, and probably in reaction to this, Cleon prosecuted Aristophanes again, this time for *xenias*—assuming citizen rights though not the son of citizens—but this prosecution, too, came to nothing. Though these attacks were (mostly) behind Aristophanes in *Clouds* (423 B.C.E.), he expresses pride in them, as he says in the play's *parabasis*:

> It was I
> who struck a blow at Cleon's paunch when he was in his
> pride . . . (583–584)[1]

Cleon died a year later while serving as general in the Battle of Amphipolis in Thrace, thus depriving Aristophanes of his favorite object of ridicule. Apart from declaring his precociousness and his animus toward Cleon, however, the *parabases* in Aristophanes's plays give us little in the way of biographical information. By the late 410s, Aristophanes started omitting *parabases* from his plays (*Lysistrata*, first produced in 411, does not have one, but *Frogs*, first produced in 405, does), and we know nothing about his later years.

Despite the obscurity of the man, his work commands respect and dominates our understanding of theatrical comedy in classical antiquity. In a career that spanned forty years (427–388 B.C.E.),

1. Aaron Poochigian, trans., *Aristophanes: Four Plays* (New York: W. W. Norton, 2021), [38].

Aristophanes composed at least forty plays, at least three of which won first prize at dramatic festivals. In a *parabasis* in *Clouds*, he criticizes his rival comedic playwrights for repackaging old material year after year and boasts of his own inventiveness:

> I'd never try to swindle you by putting out the same play two
> or three times. Furthermore, I'm good at introducing fresh
>   ideas,
> each unlike the others, all of them quite clever.
>   (*Clouds* 581–583)

Apparently, playgoers, both in fifth-century Athens and later, agreed. Not only did Aristophanes win accolades in his time, but more than a quarter of his output—eleven plays in all—has survived. A little further along in the same *parabasis* quoted above, Aristophanes prophetically anticipates his work being read in future ages:

> If you delight in me and my inventions,
> however, people in the future will remember you as wise.
>   (*Clouds* 596–597)

Given the momentous historical transitions he witnessed—the glory of Periclean Athens in his youth, the Peloponnesian War in his adulthood, and the attempted revival of Athens in his old age— and how he responded to them in his comic art, Aristophanes is a singularly important, utterly unique writer.

The Golden Age of Athens

During most of Aristophanes's lifetime, Athens was the seat of a sprawling naval empire and the great cultural center of its time. Pericles not only secured the military superiority of Athens throughout the region during his years of leadership (from 461 to 429 B.C.E.), but he also ensured that literature, art, and architecture flourished there, extending its power and influence. In 447 B.C.E. (around the time Aristophanes was born), following the Persian Wars, Pericles initiated an ambitious program to rebuild the Acropolis—the spiritual center of the city. The Parthenon, perhaps now the most famous building of all of antiquity, was mostly completed by 432 B.C.E. Vast in size and regarded as "the most perfect Doric temple ever built," it has come to symbolize the power, wealth, and culture of Athens's Golden Age.[2] The other prominent buildings visible on the Acropolis today also date to this era: the Propylaea (completed 432 B.C.E.), the Temple of Athena Nike (completed ca. 420 B.C.E.), and the Erechtheum (completed 406 B.C.E.).

This period also produced what have been traditionally regarded as the first works of history—systematic and serious inquiries into the past. In his *Histories*, Herodotus (ca. 484–425 B.C.E.) investigated the origin of the conflict between Greeks and the peoples of the East and brought his account down to his own time. Thucydides (ca. 460–400 B.C.E.), anticipating that the Peloponnesian War would be a major one, wrote a thorough and detailed account of the war from its inception. Though it originated in the sixth century B.C.E., tragedy also flourished in Athens, with tragedians such as Aeschylus (ca. 523–456 B.C.E.), Sophocles (ca. 497–405 B.C.E.), and Euripides (ca. 480–406 B.C.E.) competing at dramatic festivals for prizes. Euripides was prominent enough to be a recurring character in Aristophanes's plays, and *Frogs* features Aeschylus as a character as well.

Fifth-century Athens was also host to some of the age's leading orators and rhetoricians. Because the path to social advancement for any Athenian was through the Assembly and the law courts, there was wide demand for instruction in public speaking and persuasion. Foreign intellectuals came to Athens from throughout the region to meet that demand, sparking the so-called Sophistic Enlightenment. These men were widely sought after as tutors, but also produced bodies of work (and acolytes) that extended their influence beyond their immediate students. Protagoras of Abdera (ca. 490–420 B.C.E.), the earliest of the sophists, is known for being a religious agnostic and a relativist regarding the truth (claiming, famously, that "man is the measure of all things"). The rhetorician Gorgias of Leontini (ca. 485–390 B.C.E.) was famous for taking difficult, seemingly impossibly paradoxical positions and persuasively arguing for them—even asserting (in a lost work) for the nonexis-

2. John Julius Norwich, *Great Architecture of the World* (Boston: Da Capo, 2001), 63.

tence of Being. Another sophist, Prodicus of Ceos (ca. 465–395 B.C.E.), opened a school in Athens and gave lectures on "the correctness of names," among other subjects. Associated (somewhat unjustly) with these figures by some Athenians—and especially by Aristophanes—Socrates (ca. 470–399 B.C.E.) spent a great deal of time in the *agora* (marketplace) discussing moral philosophy, among other philosophical topics, with a group of young disciples, including Plato (429–ca. 347 B.C.E.), who later secured the fame of his teacher by writing down recollections of some of the master's provocative dialogues.

This period of prosperity and intellectual ferment, unmatched even by Renaissance Florence, came to an end in 404 B.C.E., when Athens was compelled to give up its naval empire as a consequence of losing a protracted war with Sparta.

The Peloponnesian War

The Peloponnesian War serves as the raison d'être for *Lysistrata*. An understanding of this conflict and its causes is essential for a full appreciation of the play.

Early in the fifth century, to fend off a Persian invasion (481–479 B.C.E.), the Greek states formed an alliance, the Delian League, to which allies contributed ships for a Panhellenic navy. After the war, the Athenians assumed leadership of this league and started to allow member states to pay tribute money in lieu of supplying ships and sailors. This policy served to consolidate naval power in the Athenians' hands. When Athens refused to allow member states to leave the league, it became clear that its aspirations were imperial, and the Spartans and their allies responded by forming a separate Peloponnesian League in opposition. The expansion of the Athenian Empire under the leadership of Pericles eventually caused enough friction with Sparta and its allies that Sparta felt it had no choice but to declare war.

For nearly thirty years, from 431 to 404 B.C.E. (with a short-lived peace in 421 B.C.E.), the Athenians and Spartans fought for supremacy in the Greek-speaking world. During the first decade of the conflict, known as the Archidamian War (431–421 B.C.E.), King Archidamus of Sparta annually invaded and ravaged the

Attic countryside outside Athens. These invasions caused rural residents to move inside the city walls, and the resulting overpopulation created conditions ripe for the spread of the Great Plague (430–426 B.C.E.) there. In 425 B.C.E., under the generalship of Cleon, the Athenians captured Spartan soldiers off Pylos on the island of Sphacteria. They used the threat of executing these prisoners of war as leverage to stop the annual Spartan incursions. After the Battle of Amphipolis (422 B.C.E.), in which both Cleon and the Spartan general Brasidas were killed, both sides were exhausted and ready for peace. The Athenian general Nicias and the Spartan king Pleistoanax then negotiated a treaty, the Peace of Nicias, in which each side agreed to return nearly all of the cities and territory it had taken in the war. Skirmishes soon broke out again, however, and a resumption of hostilities seemed inevitable.

In 415 B.C.E. the Athenians launched an armada to conquer Sicily under the generals Nicias, Lamachus, and Alcibiades. Since the Spartans sent troops to support some native Sicilian states, the conflict in Sicily served, in effect, as a proxy war between the Athenians and Spartans. This invasion proved a disastrous failure for the Athenians, with two of the generals dying there, and the third, Alcibiades, defecting to the Spartan side. After the collapse of the Sicilian expedition, Sparta encouraged the subject states in the Athenian Empire to revolt. Much of Ionia (now coastal Turkey) did. As a consequence of these losses, men opposed to democracy overthrew the government in Athens and established, in 411 B.C.E., an oligarchy known as "the Four Hundred," which lasted only a few months.

The following years saw the Persian Empire again become influential by providing the traditionally landlocked Spartans with ships. Eventually, the Spartans, under their general Lysander, defeated the Athenian armada at the Battle of Aegospotami in 405 B.C.E. The following year, they compelled the Athenians to surrender, requiring them to take down the city's defensive walls, disband their fleet, and accept a pro-Spartan government under thirty oligarchs known as "the Thirty." The war was over; Athens had lost. Though a band of exiled Athenians under Thrasybulus ousted the Thirty and restored democracy in 403 B.C.E., Athens never regained its former prominence.

Men and Women, Citizens and Slaves

Although in the popular imagination Athens is sometimes char-
acterized as the birthplace of democracy, we should keep important distinctions in mind. First, Athens was a radical, not a
representative, democracy: any adult male citizen could propose
measures and vote in the Assembly, the equivalent of the American legislative branch. Second, all this flourishing had a darker
side: as with all Greek states at the time, there was the large, ever-
present, and nearly voiceless population of slaves.

Although slaves occupied the lowest place in the Athenian
social hierarchy, there were still distinctions among them, with
the Scythian archers of the state police force, for example, possess-
ing greater prestige than agricultural laborers. That even middle-
class Athenians could afford slaves freed up a large segment of the
population to cultivate the arts and participate in the political
process, so a great deal of "the glory that was Greece" depended on
slave labor. As a sort of symbol of slaves' intimate relationship
with the Athenian economy, it was they who worked the lucrative
silver mines at Laurion, roughly fifty miles south of Athens, in
order to provide material for Athens's silver coinage, which in
turn financed its military adventures and great civic projects. In
Lysistrata, for example, you will encounter even the titular character speaking roughly to her Scythian slave girl—and in no way is
her behavior implied to be questionable. While in Aristophanes's
plays slaves are little more than the butt of a joke here and there,
we would do well to acknowledge that the entire edifice of the glo-
rious civilization that was fifth-century Athens, including its rich
tradition of theatrical performance, was built on a foundation of
forced, uncompensated labor. Athenians themselves may have
been willfully blind to the injustice of reserving democratic self-
determination for themselves and relegating their defeated enemies to abject servitude, but it is impossible for us now to ignore it.

Male citizens had the right to own property such as slaves and
to transact business, but they were also liable to being called up for
military service. They were able to operate both within the *polis*
(city-state) and the *oikos* (home), whereas the wives and daughters of
citizens were mostly confined to the latter. Given their confinement

and the comparative scarcity of historical evidence about them, it is striking how prominently women figure in Aristophanes's plays, as in Greek drama generally. Indeed, *Lysistrata* enacts a scenario in which women overturn the social order and seize power for themselves. A reader or playgoer might be forgiven for interpreting this fact as evidence of a rosier underlying social reality, or perhaps inferring something like proto-feminist intent on the playwright's part, but neither is true. Women in fifth-century Athens did not have suffrage, nor were they allowed to own property or represent themselves in court. A free female had to have a *kyrios* (male legal representative)—usually her father until she married, then her husband—to manage all of her social and economic relations beyond the most quotidian household duties. Respectable females only left home on special occasions, for weddings, funerals, and some religious festivals, and they are often depicted with white skin in vase paintings, because they were rarely out in the sun. There were other classes of females—*hetaerae* (courtesans), *pornoi* (prostitutes), and impoverished women, who had considerably more freedom of movement—but what they gained in mobility they paid for by being forced into more precarious, even dangerous circumstances. Respectable women were mostly limited to the roles of wife and mother, though some few could become priestesses. Their occupations were domestic, such as supervising household tasks and slaves, raising children, and making clothing. The "double standard" was even more marked in Athens ". . . than in the United States today," since, whereas husbands were free to seek sexual relations outside of the marriage, females were closely guarded.

Lysistrata gives a voice to Athenian women and a glimpse into their daily lives, but we should note that male actors played female characters as a travesty, and Aristophanes's portrayals perpetuated stereotypes about females, such as bibulousness and sex obsession. Furthermore, in order to carry out her program, Lysistrata becomes a "man-like woman" by both acting and speaking in traditionally masculine ways. For example, she and her fellow Athenians, Calonice and Myrrhine, look with the "male gaze" on the bodies of the Spartan Lampito and the representative from Boeotia. Additionally, in the blessed state at the end of the play, slaves, both male and female, remain in their oppressed position.

In the end, one can accept Lysistrata as a proto-feminist hero only with major reservations.

Theater in Athens

Aristophanes's plays were originally performed at competitive dramatic festivals called the Lenaea and the City Dionysia. Held in the winter month of Gamelium (roughly equivalent to January), the Lenaea was a religious festival in honor of Dionysus Lenaeus. The audience for this festival consisted primarily of Athenian citizens because the sea was regarded as too rough for travel. Held during the month of Elaphebolium in the spring, the City Dionysia, in contrast, accommodated a larger cosmopolitan audience. After three days of performances of tragedies there, three comedies were performed on the same day. At both of these festivals, judges representative of the ten tribes of Athens cast votes ranking the comedies in order of merit, and five of their opinions were then chosen at random to decide first, second, and third places.

In the second half of the fifth and early fourth centuries B.C.E., the Theater of Dionysus at Athens consisted simply of the south slope of the Acropolis and a roughly circular plane at its base. Temporary seats called *ikria* (planks for benches) were installed for performances. A temporary wooden backdrop called a *skēnē* was set up in the playing space. The *skēnē* usually had two doors in it for productions of comedy, and thus there were normally four ways for actors to make their entrances—through either of the doors or down one of the two side aisles (*eisodoi*). The *skēnē*, with its doors, often represented the houses of neighbors in a "middle-class" Athenian neighborhood. Thus Lysistrata at the beginning of her play greets her neighbor Myrrhine. The *skēnē* is very versatile, however— later in *Lysistrata*, for example, it represents the hill of the Acropolis itself. All productions of ancient Greek drama took place during the daytime, and there was no equivalent of modern stage lighting.

Ancient Greek drama used several contraptions that seem awkward and artificial to us. Comedy borrowed from tragedy a cantilevered crane called the *mēchanē* by which a god would often make his or her entrance "flying" (suspended by a rope). In productions of tragedy, gods were often set down on top of the *skēnē*, where they would speak down to other characters (and the audience) from "on high." Drawing on the association of this contraption with the loftier genre of tragedy, Aristophanes used it for travesty and burlesque. In *Clouds*, for example, Socrates, a mere mortal, enters on the *mēchanē* like a god and speaks, at first, in tragic pastiche. The irony is that he, allegedly a disbeliever in the traditional Greek gods, is said to "look / down on the gods" from on high (lines 260–261). In *Birds* the goddess Iris flies in on the *mēchanē* only to be threatened with violence by the mortal Peisthetaerus. Comedy also occasionally employed a narrow wooden platform on wheels called the *enkyklema*. This device was used to turn the setting inside out, that is, to roll out characters who would otherwise be concealed behind the *skēnē*.

Whereas in tragedy the setting almost always remains fixed once it is established at the beginning of the play, in comedy the setting regularly "refocuses" to a new location. In *Lysistrata* the setting shifts from Lysistrata's and Myrrhine's houses to the Acropolis. Finally, whereas the events of a tragedy are represented as taking place within a single day, scenes in comedy often take place several days after preceding scenes, so that, for example, we can see the effects of the sex strike on the men of both Athens and Sparta in *Lysistrata*.

The Play

Lysistrata was most likely produced at the Lenea in 411 B.C.E. When Aristophanes wrote the play, Athens had been fighting the Spartans, on and off, for almost twenty years. The high hopes of the Sicilian expedition had given way to near desperation in Athens. At the play's opening, an Athenian woman, Lysistrata, devises a two-part plan to end the war: first, the women of Greece will refuse to sleep with their husbands until peace is concluded, and second, the older women of Athens will seize the treasury of the Delian League (moved from Delos to the Acropolis in 454 B.C.E.). Although the Spartan representative, Lampito, is marked as "other" by her dialect, by joining Lysistrata's plan, she is absorbed into a larger sisterhood of femininity that transcends national boundaries. In fact, all distinctions in the play (except that between master and slave) work toward unification. The chorus, for example, is initially divided into equal semi-choruses of old men and old women. After staging elemental battles between fire and water, male and female, they eventually reconcile and merge into a single group.

During the confrontation between Lysistrata and the Commissioner, the feminine domestic sphere expands to become the *polis*. As females handle domestic economy, they will handle the state treasury; as females work imperfections out of a fleece, they will deal with problematic groups in the civic population:

> Imagine Athens is a fresh-shorn fleece.
> First, what you do is dunk it in a bath and wash out all
> the sheep poop; then you lay it on a bed and take a stick
> and beat out all the nasties, then you pick the thistles out.
> Next, you take those that have clumped together and become
> as thick as felt (to snag up all the civic offices)
> and comb them out and pluck their heads off. Then you go
>   and card
> the raw cleaned wool into the Basket of Reciprocal
> Agreeableness, mixing everyone in there together—
> resident aliens and other foreigners you like
> and those who owe the state back taxes—mix them in there
>   good. (604–614)

Lysistrata thus describes the *polis* as an *oikos*. During the course of the play, the former, the sphere of male action, is systematically collapsed into the latter, traditionally the purview of females.

We see the effects of the sex strike on both females and males. In scenes set several days after the opening one, Lysistrata has to prevent numerous females from running home to be with their husbands, and Harden (my translation of Cinesias, "the Arouser") arrives with an erection to claim his wife Myrrhine. He is left unsatisfied and, approached by Spartan messengers in a similar aroused state, encourages them to send ambassadors and strike a peace. The nude, voluptuous figure of Reconciliation appears, representing the lands of the Greek-speaking world, and once her parts are equitably divided up, male is reconciled with female, Spartan with Athenian. The play ends with festive songs and dances, in which the Spartan Ambassador's foreignness is appreciated.

A Note on the Translation

I translated the text of the most recent edition of this play available, that of Jeffrey Henderson, though I do occasionally attribute lines to different characters than he does.[1] With this translation I have striven to reproduce the full musical virtuosity of Aristophanes. In Greek prosody the most common and conversational meter, iambic trimeter, consists of six feet of iambs (with substitutions allowed). I render this meter as iambic pentameter in English, best known from the plays of Shakespeare. In order to preserve the modulation from this standard meter to longer lines, I translate Aristophanes's seven- and eight-stress lines into iambic heptameter and octometer, respectively.

In the Greek, sung lines (both solo and choral) are in a different dialect—Doric as opposed to Attic. To mark this change of mode, I have translated these lines into a variety of lyric meters set off by rhyme and off-rhyme. Furthermore, where choral odes break down into *Strophe* ("Turn") and *Antistrophe* ("Counter-Turn"), I preserve what is known as metrical response (the identity

---

1. Aristophanes, *Birds. Lysistrata. Women at the Thesmophoria*, Loeb Classical Library No. 179 (Cambridge, MA: Harvard University Press, 2000).

of rhythms between them), by rendering them in stanzas match-
ing in line lengths and rhyme schemes. As this translation seeks to
preserve as much of the original musical structure of the play as
possible, I have opted to provide the headings *Strophe* and *Antistrophe* in the text.

I have rendered the spoken and sung dialect of the Spartans
in *Lysistrata* as a country twang specific to no region. I use, in
addition to lexical choices, the following markers:

- *-g* dropped from gerunds and present active participles:
  runnin' for *running*
- *-n* dropped with an indefinite article before a noun beginning with a vowel: *a' honest* for *an honest*
- *a'* for *of*
- *'roun'* for *around*
- contraction *to't* for *to it*
- occasional dropped linking verbs: *you gropin'* for *you are
  groping*
- *gonna* for *going to*
- *outta* for *out of*
- *fella* for *fellow*
- *git* for *get*
- *ain't* for *isn't*
- *y'all* for the second-person plural pronoun
- *ma* for the possessive adjective *my*
- *'cause* for *because* and *jus'* for *just*
- *nekked* for *naked*
- *Mount Tayeegety* for *Mount Taygetus*

This translation, a labor of love, aspires to bring over into
English not just the "words" of Aristophanes but also his various
poetic forms, so that these two together, the words and the forms,
may re-create his meaning. I can only hope that my version
inspires the same delight in you as the Greek original does in me.

Aristophanes

Lysistrata

Characters

LYSISTRATA

CALONICE

MYRRHINE

LAMPITO

Female Representatives from Boeotia and Corinth

Scythian Slave Girl

OLD MEN'S CHORUS LEADER *(Draces)*

CHORUS OF OLD MEN

OLD WOMEN'S CHORUS LEADER *(Stratyllis)*

CHORUS OF OLD WOMEN

COMMISSIONER

Four Policemen

Four Scythian Archers

Three Old Women

Four Women

HARDEN

Manes The Slave

BABY

SPARTAN MESSENGER

Two Spartan Ambassadors

Two Athenian Ambassadors

Reconciliation

ATHENIAN DOORKEEPER

SLAVES

PIPER

Lysistrata
(Lysistrate)

First produced in 411 B.C.E.

(*The setting is Athens, Greece, in 411 B.C.E. Athens has been at war with Sparta and other Greek states, including Boeotia and Corinth, on and off for almost twenty years. There is a backdrop with two doors in it, for the moment representing the fronts of two typical Athenian houses. Lysistrata emerges through one of the doors. It is very early in the morning.*)

LYSISTRATA
If all the women had been called to worship
Pan, Bacchus or the Goddesses of Sex
at Colias,° believe me, there would be
so many drums around you couldn't move,
and now there's not a single female here—

(*Calonice emerges from the other door.*)

except my neighbor coming out. Good morning,
Calonice.

CALONICE
                    Morning, Lysistrata.
What's wrong with you? Don't look so grumpy, girl.
Scrunching your face up like a tight-drawn bow
is hardly an attractive look for you.   10

LYSISTRATA
Oh, but my heart's on fire. I'm grieving over
the way we women have been treated. Men
think we are all so wicked.

CALONICE
                    Aren't we, though?

LYSISTRATA
I told the girls to come on time to talk
about important business, but they're late.
They must be sleeping.

CALONICE
                              Sweetie, they'll be here.
It's tough, you know, for wives to get away—
one will be doting on her man; another
waking the slaves. While one of them is putting
the baby down, another will be nursing   20
or giving baths.

LYSISTRATA
                    But there's another matter
far more important to them than such things.

CALONICE
What is it, Lysistrata? Why have you
convened this female council here today?
Is it a big deal?

LYSISTRATA
                    Yes, it's big.

CALONICE
                              And meaty?

LYSISTRATA
Meaty. Yes.

CALONICE
                    Why aren't the women here, then?

LYSISTRATA
That's not my meaning. They'd have been here quick
enough for *that*. But there's this other thing
I've hit on; I've been tossing it about
for many sleepless nights.

CALONICE

                              "Tossing" the thing—   30
by now it must be flimsy.

LYSISTRATA

                    Yes, so "flimsy"
that all of Greece's future rests upon
us women.

CALONICE

            On us women! Then it rests
on very little.

LYSISTRATA

            Yes, the city's future
rests upon womankind. Or else the people
of southern Greece will wholly cease to be—

CALONICE

It would be better if they did, by Zeus!

LYSISTRATA

. . . and all of the Boeotians be destroyed—

CALONICE

But not their eels, but not their precious eels!°

LYSISTRATA

. . . and Athens, but I don't dare utter such   40
an end for Athens. You must guess my meaning.
If the women would just meet here now,
all of them from the South and from Boeotia
and greater Athens, we could save all Greece!

CALONICE

But what can women do that's excellent
or noble? We just sit around at home

looking all pretty in our saffron dresses,
makeup, cambric gowns, and cozy shoes.

LYSISTRATA
Those are the very things I hope will save us—
our little saffron gowns, perfumes, and shoes,   50
our rouge and see-through undergarments.

CALONICE
                                        How, though?

LYSISTRATA
They will make it so that no man living
will ever lift a spear against another . . .

CALONICE
Then, by Demeter and Persephone,°
I'm heading out to have a dress dyed saffron!

LYSISTRATA
. . . or hold a shield . . .

CALONICE
                        I'll wear a cambric gown!

LYSISTRATA
. . . or even a knife.

CALONICE
                        I'm off to go shoe shopping!

LYSISTRATA
I know! Shouldn't they all have come by now?

CALONICE
"Come," no—they should have *flown* here hours ago.

LYSISTRATA

    Dear, you will find that they are perfectly   60
    Athenian—always later than they should be.°
    There aren't even any who have sailed
    over from Salamis or the Paralia.°

CALONICE

    Those girls must still be mounted on their broad-beamed
    dinghies.

LYSISTRATA

            Not even the Acharnian women°
    are here. I thought they'd be the first to come.
    I counted on them.

CALONICE

                Theogenes's wife,
    at least, had raised her mainsail high to get here.°

(*Women enter from stage right.*)

    But look—some of the girls are coming now.

(*More women enter from stage left, including Myrrhine.*)

LYSISTRATA

    And there are more arriving on this side.   70

CALONICE

    They reek! Where have they come from?

LYSISTRATA

                      Stinkydale.°

CALONICE

    Of course: they kicked the stink up when they came.

MYRRHINE
  What's up, Lysistrata? Are we tardy?
  What do you have to tell us? Why so quiet?

LYSISTRATA
  Myrrhine, I disapprove of your arriving
  so late when there is such important business.

MYRRHINE
  It was so dark at home. I couldn't find
  my bra. We're here now. Give us what you've got.

LYSISTRATA
  No, we should wait a bit until the women
  come in from Boeotia and the South.   80

MYRRHINE
  That's better, yes.

(*Lampito enters from stage right, with the Female Representatives from Boeotia and Corinth and several other females. She speaks with a southern twang.*)

                                    But look, here comes Lampito!

LYSISTRATA
  Lampito darling, here you are from Sparta.
  Sweetie, why, how gorgeous you are looking!
  Your skin is glowing, and your body's ripped.
  I bet that you could snap a bull's neck.

LAMPITO
                                    Shee-ute,
  I bet I could. I work out regular—
  you know, those heel-to-butt kicks people do.

CALONICE (*groping Lampito's breasts*)
  Wow, what a banging rack you have!

LAMPITO

                                        Whoa, now!
You gropin' me like I'm some animal
you gonna sacrifice.

LYSISTRATA

                          And this girl here,   90
where is she from?

LAMPITO

                          She come here representin'
Boeotia.

MYRRHINE

            With her undulating lowlands,
she looks just like Boeotia!

CALONICE

                          Yes indeed.

(*looking down the Boeotian Representative's dress at her pubic hair*)

Look at that well-cropped herbage.

LYSISTRATA

                          Who's this woman?

LAMPITO

She's a great, great lady, outta Corinth.

CALONICE

She's great alright! Great front and great behind!

LAMPITO

Now, which a' y'all called for this here meetin'?

LYSISTRATA

I am the one.

LAMPITO
                    Then go on, girl. You tell us
what you got to say.

CALONICE
                    Yes, darling, please
do tell us what this serious business is.   100

LYSISTRATA
I want to tell you but, before I do,
let me put a little question to you.

CALONICE
Ask away.

LYSISTRATA
          Don't all you ladies miss
your children's fathers when they're on campaign?
Each of you has a husband who's away—
I know you do.

CALONICE
                    Five months my man's been gone
up north in Thrace fighting to save Eucrates
the general.°

MYRRHINE
                    Seven months my man's been off
at Pylos.°

LAMPITO
          Heck, my man no quicker comes
back home to Sparta than he up and straps   110
his shield on and is gone again.

CALONICE
                              What's worse,
there aren't even any lover-boys

to have affairs with. And, ever since Miletus
broke away from us, I haven't seen
one of those five-inch dildos,° no, not one,
though they'd have been small consolation to us.

LYSISTRATA

Ladies, if I could come up with a way
to end the war, would you agree to join me?

CALONICE

By Demeter and Persephone,
I would agree, though I be forced to sell   120
this gown and on the same day blow the money
getting . . . drunk!

MYRRHINE

              Count me in, also. I'd
be cut right down the middle like a flounder
and donate half myself to help you out.

LAMPITO

I'd climb Mount Tayeegety° if I thought
I'd catch a glimmer a' a peace from there.

LYSISTRATA

I'll tell you, then. No need to keep the secret.
Alright: If we are going to force our men
to make a treaty, then we must abstain from . . .

CALONICE

What is it? Tell us.

LYSISTRATA

              You will do it, then?   130

CALONICE

Yes, though we have to sacrifice our lives!

LYSISTRATA
  Alright, then. What we must abstain from is . . .
  dick.

(*All the women turn away from Lysistrata, some shaking
their heads, some weeping.*)

          Hold on, don't turn away from me.
  Where are you going? Don't pout and shake your heads.
  Why are you turning pale? Why shedding tears?
  Will you or won't you do this thing? Decide.

CALONICE
  I just can't do it. Let the war go on.

MYRRHINE
  God no, me either. Let the war go on.

LYSISTRATA (*to Myrrhine*)
  You, too, Ms. Flounderfish? Weren't you just saying
  that you would cut yourself in half for peace?   140

MYRRHINE
  Anything else I'd do! If it'd help,
  I'd walk through fire. Just, no, no, not the dick.
  There's nothing like it, dear.

LYSISTRATA
                              Are you out, too?

WOMAN
  Me? I would also rather walk through fire.

LYSISTRATA
  What a bunch of nymphos women are!
  The tragedies they make about our sex
  are true, since all we do is hump and dump.°

But you, my Spartan friend—if you alone
are with me, then we still might save this business.
Vote with me!

LAMPITO

                It ain't no fun for women   150
to sleep without a woody for companion;
still, I'm with you 'cause we need the peace.

LYSISTRATA

You are a perfect dear! The one true woman!

CALONICE

Hey, now, even if we did abstain from . . .
from what you said (and may we never have to),
would peace be then more likely to occur?

LYSISTRATA

Sure it would. If we lounged about the house
with makeup on and sauntered past our husbands
wearing no clothes except a see-through gown
and trimmed our pubes into a perfect triangle,   160
and if the men, then, got all hard and burned
to screw us, but we backed off and refused
to touch them, they would cut a peace damn quick.
You can be sure of that.

LAMPITO

                     Like Menelaus.
When he caught sight a' nekked Helen's peaches,
lickety-split he threw his sword aside.°

CALONICE

What happens if our husbands just ignore us?

LYSISTRATA

Well, like a poet says somewhere: In dog days,
dildo away.°

CALONICE
            Faux boners are a joke!
And, anyway, what if our men just drag us   170
into the bedroom?

LYSISTRATA
                        Hold onto the door frame.

CALONICE
What if they beat us up?

LYSISTRATA
                              Then grudgingly
submit. Men get no pleasure out of screwing
when they have to make a woman do it,
and there are other ways to make men ache.
They will surrender to us soon, I promise.
No man can live a happy life unless
his wife allows it.

CALONICE (*to Lampito and Lysistrata*)
                        Well, if this seems best
to you two girls, the rest of us agree.

LAMPITO
We Spartan girls can surely git *our* men   180
to make a' honest sort a' peace that's good
for everyone. But how can anybody
keep your Athenian mob from acting like
the crazy folk they are?

LYSISTRATA
                        I promise you
that we will bring our husbands round to peace.

LAMPITO
Y'all can't—with all them warships under sail
and tons a' money in Athena's temple.°

LYSISTRATA
That issue has been taken care of. We
are going to occupy the hilltop fortress
of the Acropolis this very morning.°   190
That task has fallen to the older women.
Even as we are working out the terms
of our agreement here, they, on the pretext
of making sacrifice, are up there taking
the citadel.

LAMPITO
                    Well, now, that sounds jus' right,
like all the things you've said to me so far.

LYSISTRATA
Why don't we swear an oath right now, Lampito,
so that the details will be fixed forever?

LAMPITO
Lay down the oath, so y'all and I can swear it.

LYSISTRATA
Very well. Where is my Scythian slave girl?   200

(*The Scythian Slave Girl enters, carrying a shield.*)

What are you gaping at? Now put the shield
facedown there on the ground in front of us,
and someone bring the cuttings from the victim.

(*The Slave Girl lays the shield facedown on the stage.*)

CALONICE
What sort of oath will we be swearing for you?

LYSISTRATA
What sort of oath? The oath that I have heard
Aeschylus had his heroes swear to, after
they slit a victim's throat above a shield.°

CALONICE
Come on, Lysistrata, please don't make us
swear an oath for peace upon a shield!

LYSISTRATA
What should the oath be, then?

CALONICE
                              What if we got   210
a pure-white steed somewhere and cut it up?°

LYSISTRATA
A pure-white steed?

CALONICE
                    Well, then, how will we swear?

LYSISTRATA
I'll tell you what I think: Let's put a big
black wine cup on the ground right here, top upward,
and sacrifice a jar of Thasian wine into it
and swear never to add a drop of water.°

LAMPITO
Yee-haw! I can't praise that oath enough!

LYSISTRATA
Someone go in and bring the cup and jar.

(*The Slave Girl fetches a wine cup and wine jar from offstage.*)

MYRRHINE
O my dear ladies, that's a whole wine vat!

CALONICE
We could get wasted just by touching it.   220

LYSISTRATA (*pretending the wine cup is a sacrificial boar*)
  Put down the wine cup now, and everyone
  come lay her hands upon this sacral—boar.

(*She prays while pouring wine from the jar into the cup.*)

  O Queen Persuasion and O Cup of Mirth,
  kindly accept this offering from women.

CALONICE
  The blood looks good and bubbles like it should.

LAMPITO
  It smells a' sweetness, by the gods.

MYRRHINE

                              Please, ladies,
  let me be first!

CALONICE
                    By Aphrodite, only
  if your number's up.

LYSISTRATA
                    Hey there, Lampito,
  everyone, lay your hands upon the wine cup.
  One of you will repeat, for all, the terms   230
  of our agreement after me, and then
  the rest will swear to keep them once we're done.

No man, be he a lover or a husband . . .

CALONICE (*stepping up as the representative for all the women*)
  No man, be he a lover or a husband . . .

LYSISTRATA
  . . . shall come up to me with a boner. Say it!

CALONICE
. . . shall come up to me with a boner.
                                                    Ah!
My knees are going to buckle, Lysistrata!

LYSISTRATA
And I shall pass the time in celibacy . . .

CALONICE
And I shall pass the time in celibacy . . .

LYSISTRATA
. . . dressed in a saffron gown and all made up . . .   240

CALONICE
. . . dressed in a saffron gown and all made up . . .

LYSISTRATA
. . . so that my man gets very hot for me.

CALONICE
. . . so that my man gets very hot for me.

LYSISTRATA
Never shall I consent to sex with him.

CALONICE
Never shall I consent to sex with him.

LYSISTRATA
And if he forces me against my will . . .

CALONICE
And if he forces me against my will . . .

LYSISTRATA
. . . I shall be frigid and shall not grind back.

CALONICE
. . . I shall be frigid and shall not grind back . . .

LYSISTROPO.54ATA
. . . *nor raise my fancy slippers toward the ceiling* . . .   250

CALONICE
. . . nor raise my fancy slippers toward the ceiling . . .

LYSISTRATA
. . . *nor pose my haunches like a lioness's.*

CALONICE
. . . nor pose my haunches like a lioness's.

LYSISTRATA
If I fulfill these vows, may I drink wine . . .

CALONICE
If I fulfill these vows, may I drink wine . . .

LYSISTRATA
. . . *but, if I fail, this cup be full of water.*

CALONICE
. . . but, if I fail, this cup be full of water.

LYSISTRATA
So do you women swear?

ALL THE WOMEN
                              So do we swear.

LYSISTRATA
By drinking from this cup, I consecrate it.

(*Lysistrata takes a deep drink.*)

CALONICE (*eager to take her drink*)
  Only your portion, dear. Prove from the start   260
  that we are allies.

(*Shouts are heard from offstage. They are the sound of older
woman seizing the Acropolis.*)

LAMPITO
                    What's that hullabaloo?

LYSISTRATA
  That's what I was explaining to you: women
  have just now taken the Acropolis,
  Athena's hilltop fortress. Now, Lampito,
  head home and see to your side of this business—
  just leave these women here as hostages.

(*Lampito exits, stage right, with the Representatives from
Boeotia and Corinth, leaving several females behind.*)

  We, for our part, will march into the fortress
  and help the other women bar the gates.

CALONICE
  But don't you think the men will very quickly
  march in arms against us?

LYSISTRATA
                    Have no fear.   270
  Never will they muster threat or fire
  enough to penetrate our gates unless
  they give in to our terms.

CALONICE
                    By Aphrodite,
  they won't get in, or else we women never
  should wear the names of "nasty" and "impossible."

(*The setting refocuses from the houses of Lysistrata and Calonice
to the Acropolis. The two doors now represent the Propylaea, or
gates to the Acropolis. Lysistrata and the remaining women exit
through a stage door. A Chorus of Old Men enter from stage
right, carrying small branches and a smoking pot full of coals.*)

CHORUS OF OLD MEN
Lead on, Draces,° lead on, though your shoulder's aching bad
under that very heavy load of fresh-green olivewood.

> *Strophe 1*
> There will be lots of shocks in lives as long as ours.
> Who would have thought we'd hear that
>   womankind,
> a race we nursed at home, a blatant curse,   280
> would now control Athena's statue and
> my beautiful Acropolis and, even worse,
> have sealed the fortress gates with bolts and bars?

Let's hurry to the citadel as quick as we can go
and make a ring of timber round the women, all those who
have spawned or nurtured this revolt. Let's make a giant pile
of wood, a bonfire, and proceed, with a united will
and torches in our hands, to immolate them, all of them—
and Lycon's drunken wife° should be the first to feel the flame!

> *Antistrophe 1*
> Their sex won't get to mock me while I'm drawing
>   breath.   290
> Cleomenes,° the first to occupy
> that citadel, barely escaped alive.
> Though Spartan-proud, he gave his spear to me
> and slunk off, small-cloaked, starved, in sore need of
>   a shave.
> It had been six years since he had a bath.

Such was the dogged way that we besieged the man—no sleep
by day or night, we stood in ranks seventeen-shieldmen deep.

And now am I just going to do nothing, stand around
instead of chastening the insolence of womankind,
the foes of every godhead, and Euripides as well?°   300
May Marathon no longer feature my memorial.°

> *Strophe 2*
> We're almost there. All that remains, now, is that
>   steep
> stretch to the citadel—my goal, my hope.
> But, oh, without a donkey, how the heck
> will we move all this lumber to that height?
> For all this pair of tree trunks weighs my shoulders
>   down,
> I must bear up, I must go on,
> and keep my fire alight.
> It must keep burning till I reach the top.
>
> Huff, puff, and alack,   310
> the smoke!
>
> *Antistrophe 2*
> Great Lord Heracles!° The smoke has viciously
> leapt from the bucket and come after me.
> My eyes sting from its crazy bitch attack.
> No doubt ours is the Lemnian sort of fire°—
> that's why it's murdering my bloodshot eyes like this.
> On, on to the Acropolis!
> Rush to Athena, rescue her!
> It's urgent: we must save the deity!
>
> Huff, puff, and alack,   320
> the smoke!

Thanks to the gods, the fire is very much alive and kicking.
Come on, let's set our loads of wood down here. Then, after
   sticking
the torches in the pail and seeing that they catch a flame,
let's rush the gates like battering rams. If, when we order them

to yield, the women still refuse, we'll set the gates on fire
and smoke the rebels out. Alright, then, put the logs down
   there.
That smoke is something. Damn. Hey, generals at the naval
   base
in Samos, do you want to help us stack this lumber?°

(*The Chorus of Old Men set the branches down.*)

                                        Those

at last are off my back! Now, fire pail, it is up to you   330
to rouse your embers and provide me with a bright
   flambeau.
Victory Goddess Nike,° be our ally, fight with us,
and we will win a trophy over female brazenness.

(*A Chorus of Old Women enter through a stage door. They
are carrying jugs full of water.*)

CHORUS OF OLD WOMEN
I think that I see smoke and ash, like something is aflame.
Faster now, my female soldiers. Hurry. Double time.

> *Strophe 1*
> Soar, women, soar up there before
> our fighting sisters have been set on fire.
> Look how the fierce winds fan the blaze!
> Those old men would commit atrocities
> against us. I am terribly afraid   340
> we are too late to do the others any good.
>
> I've just come from the well,
> where I had trouble filling up this water jug.
> Yes, in the predawn ruckus and the glug-glug-glug
> and clay-pot clash and shatter of it all,
> I fought a tattooed slave and serving maid
> and boldly set this vessel on my head
> and now, to save my sister rebels from
> the threatened fiery demise, have come,
> bringing lots of liquid aid.   350

Antistrophe 1
I've heard that homicidal old
fogeys have been let loose into the wild.
Dragging a superhuman weight
of firewood up the slope, they shout and shout,
like stokers in a bathhouse steam room, rash
threats like "We're gonna turn those nasty hags to
    ash."

Goddess Athena, please,
let me not see my sisters roasting in the fire.
I want to see them save from craziness and war
our fellow citizens and all of Greece.   360
Yes, Golden-Crested Fortress Guardian,°
that is why we have occupied your shrine.
Tritogeneia,° aid us in this fight
and, if a man's hand sets your house alight,
help us pour the water on.

OLD WOMEN'S CHORUS LEADER (*seeing the Chorus of Old Men for the first time*)
    Halt, women! What is this? They must be execrable villains
    because no good and pious men would do what they are doing.

OLD MEN'S CHORUS LEADER
    Here is a difficulty we did not expect to see:
    a swarm of them has come out of the gates to help the others.

OLD WOMEN'S CHORUS LEADER
    What, are you frightened? Does it seem that there are lots
        of us?   370
    Well, you are only seeing one small fraction of our horde.

OLD MEN'S CHORUS LEADER
    Men, are we going to let these women yammer on like this?
    Someone should take his log and just start walloping them
        good.

OLD WOMEN'S CHORUS LEADER
We'd better put our pitchers down so that our hands are free
in case one of those good-for-nothings lays his hands on us.

(*The Chorus of Old Women set down the pitchers.*)

OLD MEN'S CHORUS LEADER
By Zeus, if someone socked them in their kissers two or
     three times—
you know, like Bupe-Bupe-Bupalus,° they would be much
     more quiet.

OLD WOMEN'S CHORUS LEADER
Well, here's my kisser. Hit me. I can take it. If you do, though,
no other bitch will ever grab you by the balls again!

OLD MEN'S CHORUS LEADER
Shut up, or I will knock you right out of your withered
     hide.   380

OLD WOMEN'S CHORUS LEADER
Come on and touch me, touch Stratyllis with your fingertip.

OLD MEN'S CHORUS LEADER
If I used combo punches, what you got to get me back?

OLD WOMEN'S CHORUS LEADER
I'd use my teeth to rip your lungs and bowels out of your body.

OLD MEN'S CHORUS LEADER
I swear, no poet's wiser than Euripides. He said:
"No race of beasts exists as pitiless as womankind."

OLD WOMEN'S CHORUS LEADER
Come on, let's pick our water pitchers up and get them ready.

(*The Chorus of Old Women pick up the pitchers.*)

OLD MEN'S CHORUS LEADER
Harridan hateful to the gods, why did you come with water?

OLD WOMEN'S CHORUS LEADER
Why did you come with fire, you burial mound? To burn your carcass?

OLD MEN'S CHORUS LEADER
No, to build a big bonfire and burn up all your friends.

OLD WOMEN'S CHORUS LEADER
And I, well, I have come to put that fire out with my water.   390

OLD MEN'S CHORUS LEADER
You think you're going to douse my fire?

OLD WOMEN'S CHORUS LEADER
                              You'll find out soon enough.

OLD MEN'S CHORUS LEADER
I think I might just use this torch to roast you where you stand.

OLD WOMEN'S CHORUS LEADER
Happen to bring some soap along? I'm giving you a bath.

OLD MEN'S CHORUS LEADER
A bath from you, a shriveled hag?

OLD WOMEN'S CHORUS LEADER
                              And you, you're quite a bridegroom.

OLD MEN'S CHORUS LEADER (*to the Chorus of Old Men*)
You hear that disrespect?

OLD WOMEN'S CHORUS LEADER
                              I'm free, and I will speak my mind!

OLD MEN'S CHORUS LEADER
I'll make you quit your screeching!

OLD WOMEN'S CHORUS LEADER
                                    You aren't on a jury now!°

OLD MEN'S CHORUS LEADER (*to the Chorus of Old Men*)
Set her hair on fire!

OLD WOMEN'S CHORUS LEADER (*pouring water onto the
Old Men's Chorus Leader*)
                                    Do your work, now, River God.

(*The Chorus of Old Women pour water on the Chorus of Old
Men.*)

OLD MEN'S CHORUS LEADER
Oh no!

OLD WOMEN'S CHORUS LEADER (*ironically*)
        I hope it didn't scald you.

OLD MEN'S CHORUS LEADER
Scald me? Desist! What are you doing?

OLD WOMEN'S CHORUS LEADER
I'm watering you so you bloom.   400

OLD MEN'S CHORUS LEADER
I'm dry again from shivering.

OLD WOMEN'S CHORUS LEADER
Well, since you have a fire, why not sit down and warm
    yourself?

(*The Commissioner of Athens enters from stage left. He has
four Policemen with him and four Scythian Archers. They are
all wearing disproportionately large, flaccid strap-on penises.*)

COMMISSIONER

Has feminine licentiousness flared up
again? The kettledrums? The endless cries
to that exotic god Sabezius?°
And all that rooftop worship of Adonis°
I heard while sitting once in the Assembly?
Demostratus (the villain) was proposing
that we dispatch a fleet to Sicily,
and all the while his wife would not stop dancing   410
and shouting, "Oh Adonis! Oh!" Demostratus,
next, was proposing we conscript foot soldiers
out of Zacynthus,° and his wife just kept on
drinking on the rooftop and exclaiming,
"Beat your bosoms for Adonis!" Well,
that god-detested wretched Captain Blather
just went on legislating, while his wife
exhibited the sort of wild behavior
you get from womankind.

OLD MEN'S CHORUS LEADER (*gesturing to the Chorus
of Old Women*)

                              What will you say
when you find out about *these* ladies' cheek?   420
They've gone too far in every way. They've even
soaked us with those jugs of theirs. We stand here
shaking our clothes out like we've pissed ourselves!

COMMISSIONER

By Poseidon,° we've been asking for it!
We ourselves incite our wives' transgressions;
we positively *teach* them to be wanton,
and so it's no surprise these sorts of plots
are growing up among them. We ourselves
go to the shops and say such things as:

                              "Goldsmith,
you know that necklace that I had you make?   430
Last evening, while my wife was dancing in it,
the post that's on the fastener slipped out of

the hole. Now I am off to Salamis—
gone till tomorrow. If you have the time,
stop by my house this evening, please, and fit
a post into her hole."
                              Another husband goes
to see a shoemaker, a teenage boy
who's got a grown man's cock, and says such things as:
"Shoemaker, there's this strap that's rubbing raw
my darling's pinkie toe. Please come around   440
some early afternoon and stretch her gap out
wider."
            That's the licentiousness that's led us
to this impasse where I, the great Commish,
when I need money from the treasury
to outfit ships with oars, can't get inside
because I'm locked out by our women!

(*to the Policemen and Scythian Archers*)

                                          You,
what good is standing there? Go get some crowbars.
I'm going to put an end to female brashness
once and for all!

(*to a Policeman*)

                    What are you gaping at,
you dope? The only thing you're looking for's   450
a tavern, I suspect.

(*to the Policemen and Scythian Archers*)

                    All of you, come, now,
drive the crowbars underneath the gates
and yank from there, and I'll start yanking mine
from over here.

(*The males onstage start prying at one of the stage doors with
the crowbars. Lysistrata enters from the other stage door. She
is wearing a head scarf. Three Old Women attend, carrying
a wreath, ribbons, and a basket containing wool and a
spindle.*)

LYSISTRATA
>   Stop yanking on those things.
> I'm coming out all on my own. Besides,
> what need is there for crowbars? What you need
> are wits and brains.

COMMISSIONER
>   Oh really? What a bitch!
> Where's a policeman?

(*to the First Policeman*)

>   Go and get her. Bind
> her hands behind her back.

LYSISTRATA
>   Yeah, if that man
> dares touch me even with a fingertip,   460
> I'll send him home, a state employee, weeping.

(*The First Policeman refuses to grab Lysistrata.*)

COMMISSIONER (*to the First Policeman*)
> What, are you scared of her?

(*to the Second Policeman*)

>   Go help him. Quick, now,
> grab her around the waist and bind her hands.

FIRST OLD WOMAN (*to the Second Policeman*)
> If you so much as lay a hand on her,
> I'll hit you so hard that you shit yourself!

(*The Second Policeman refuses to grab Lysistrata.*)

COMMISSIONER
> "Shit himself"? Where's my other officer?

(*to the Third Policeman*)

> You, come and tie this foul-mouthed hag up first.

SECOND OLD WOMAN (*to the Third Policeman*)
Touch her, and you'll be begging for a cup°
to be warmed up to soothe your big black eye.

(*The Third Policeman refuses to grab the First Old Woman.*)

COMMISSIONER
What *is* this?

(*to the Fourth Policeman*)

Hey there, you, policeman, seize her.   470
I'll stop those hags from charging from the gates.

THIRD OLD WOMAN (*to the Fourth Policeman*)
Go on and touch her, do it, and I'll rip
your hair out by the roots and leave you screaming.

(*The Fourth Policeman refuses to grab the First Old Woman.
All four Policemen run off, stage left.*)

COMMISSIONER
Dammit! Now I've got no policemen left.
All the same, men must never be defeated
by women. Form up, Scythians, and charge them!

(*The four Scythian Archers form in a line.*)

LYSISTRATA
You will soon learn well that we have four
brigades of fighting women on reserve
inside the gates.

COMMISSIONER
Scythians, wrench their hands
behind their backs!

LYSISTRATA
March out, O my reservists!   480

(*Women march out of the stage door in military formation.*)

Onward, my greens-'n'-egg-seed-market-mongers,
my tavern-keeping-bread-'n'-garlic-hawkers!
Take them down! Wallop them! Devastate
and mock them! Be as foul as you can be!

(*After a mock battle, the Scythian Archers retreat.*)

Stop now! Withdraw. Don't wait to strip the corpses.°

COMMISSIONER

Goodness! My Scythians have not fared well.

LYSISTRATA

What did you think would happen? Did you think
you'd be attacking slave girls? Did you think
that women have no fight in them?

COMMISSIONER

                                    Yes, lots,
so long as someone nearby serves them drinks.   490

OLD MEN'S CHORUS LEADER (*to the Commissioner*)

Commissioner, you just keep gabbing on and on and wasting
   words.
Why would you try to come to terms with savage beasts like
   these?
Do you not understand the sort of bath we got just now?
They left our cloaks all sopping, and they never gave us soap!

OLD WOMEN'S CHORUS LEADER (*to the Commissioner*)

Buddy, you can't just hit a person anytime you want.
Plus, if you do attack me, you will wind up with a black eye.
I'd rather be at home, seated demurely like a maiden,
troubling no one, crushing not one blade of grass—except,
if someone riles me like a wasp's nest, I will be a wasp.

CHORUS OF OLD MEN

> *Strophe*
> Great Lord Zeus, what are we going to do about
>   this pack   500

of monsters? They are unendurable. Come, now,
  and look
into this plot along with me until
we know why they have seized the citadel
and the whole sacred and restricted space
that is our great limestone Acropolis.

OLD MEN'S CHORUS LEADER
Now start the inquisition! Cast suspicion upon all
she says. It's shameful that we let these actions go unchecked.

COMMISSIONER
Here is the thing I want to find out first of all, by Zeus:
What did you hope to gain by locking up the citadel?

LYSISTRATA
To keep the money safe and stop the war for lack of it.   510

COMMISSIONER
We are at war because of money—is that what you think?

LYSISTRATA
Yes, and that's why so many other things got screwed up, too.
Pisander and the other would-be officeholders kept on
stirring up trouble as a pretext to get at the silver.
Now they can keep on stirring up whatever they might scheme—
they will be taking no more money from the citadel.

COMMISSIONER
What are you going to do with it?

LYSISTRATA

                              We'll manage it, of course.

COMMISSIONER
Women will manage it?

LYSISTRATA
                    Why do you think that this is strange?
Don't we already manage your domestic finances?

COMMISSIONER
That's not the same.

LYSISTRATA
                    Why not?

COMMISSIONER
                          This money is for waging war.   520

LYSISTRATA
There doesn't need to be a war.

COMMISSIONER
                          How will we be protected?

LYSISTRATA
We women will protect you.

COMMISSIONER
                          What, you women?

LYSISTRATA
                                Yes, us women.

COMMISSIONER
How ballsy.

LYSISTRATA
We will save you whether you consent or not.

COMMISSIONER
That's crazy talk!

LYSISTRATA
> Oh, are you angry? Still it must be done.

COMMISSIONER
It's just not proper.

LYSISTRATA
> Still, you must be saved, my dear, dear man.

COMMISSIONER
Even if I never asked?

LYSISTRATA
> Yes, all the more for that.

COMMISSIONER
But why are peace and war of such importance to you now?

LYSISTRATA
I'll tell you.

COMMISSIONER (*threatening her with his fist*)
> Do it quick or else you're going to get beaten.

LYSISTRATA
Listen up, then, and control your hands.

COMMISSIONER
> I can't control them.
I'm so worked up that I can't keep from flailing.

FIRST OLD WOMAN (*to the Commissioner*)
> You're the one   530
who's gonna get a beating!

COMMISSIONER (*to the First Old Woman*)
> Croak away, you old hag, croak!

(*to Lysistrata*)

And you there, start explaining what you plan to do.

LYSISTRATA
                                        With pleasure:
Blessed with self-control, we women have endured in silence,
for quite a long time now, whatever you men did, because
you never let us speak. Believe me: you weren't all we dreamed
    of—
yes, we took good stock of you. Quite frequently at home
we heard you speaking of some fool political decision
you'd lately made. Then, full of agony but still all smiles,
we'd ask: "What was resolved about the rider to the peace
today in the Assembly?" Well, my husband always
    answered,   540
"What's it to you?" and "Woman, shut your mouth." And I
    shut up—

FIRST OLD WOMAN
Not me: I never would have shut my mouth.

COMMISSIONER (*to the First Old Woman*)
                                        Well, if you hadn't,
you'd have gotten smacked.

LYSISTRATA
                                ... I shut up, and I stayed at home.
And soon enough we heard about some even more atrocious
legislation you had passed. And I would say, "O husband,
why have you gone and voted in so very bad a law?"
Frowningly he would snap back: "Mind your spinning, now,
    or else
I'll knock your head around, some. *War is an affair for men.*"°

COMMISSIONER
Yeah, by the gods, your husband schooled you good!

LYSISTRATA
                              What's "good," moron,
about not giving good advice to people who are making   550
awful decisions? When we heard you men all over town
lamenting, "Isn't there a *man* left anywhere in Athens?"
and others crying, "No *men* left," we women met in council,
and we resolved to raise a coup and rescue Greece ourselves.
Why should we waste more time? If you are ready now to
  shut up
just like you said "shut up" to us and heed our good advice,
we'll tell you how to set the city straight.

COMMISSIONER
                              You? You tell *us*?
An outrage! It's impossible!

LYSISTRATA
                    Shut up.

COMMISSIONER
                    "Shut up" for *you*,
a nasty creature with a veil on? Never, on my life!

LYSISTRATA (*taking her head scarf off and putting it on the
Commissioner*)
  Well, if my veil's the trouble here,   560
  you take it from me, wear it over
  your head. Now you're the "shut up" one.

FIRST OLD WOMAN (*handing the Commissioner a sewing
basket*)
  Oh, and here's a sewing basket.

LYSISTRATA
  Tuck in your clothes and get some beans
  to chew on° while you do your spinning.
  War is an affair for women.

OLD WOMEN'S CHORUS LEADER
  Leave your water jugs, now, girls, because the time has come
  for us to play our part by helping in a different way.

(*The Chorus of Old Women set down the pitchers.*)

CHORUS OF OLD WOMEN
          Strophe
          I'll never tire of dancing. I'll keep dancing on and on,
          and no exhausting hours of work will make my knees
              break down.   570
          I'm not afraid of anything because
          I've women with me who are bold as these.
          They've got good breeding, grace and spunk in them.
          They've got street smarts and patriotic vim.

  Now most manly grannies, ye maternal stinging jellies,
  advance with rage and don't grow soft. Run with a gale astern.

LYSISTRATA
  If sweet-souled Eros and his mother Aphrodite of Cyprus
  breathe desire onto our breasts and thighs, if they afflict
  the men with big love-clubs of amorous rigidity,
  all Greece will come to praise us as the "Looseners of War."   580

COMMISSIONER
  And why's that?

LYSISTRATA
          First we will have put a stop to armed men going
  around the market and behaving like they're crazy people.

FIRST OLD WOMAN
  Three cheers for Aphrodite!

LYSISTRATA
                    At this moment, in the market,

among the pottery stalls and grocers, there are men with
  weapons
walking around like nutjobs.

COMMISSIONER
Men are best when they look manly.

LYSISTRATA
It's madness when a soldier with a Gorgon on his shield
goes fresh-fish shopping.

FIRST OLD WOMAN
                Yes, I saw a mounted man with long hair,
a cavalry commander, buying oatmeal from a woman—
he had her scoop the stuff into his metal helmet! Plus,
this Thracian guy would not stop brandishing his shield
  and lance   590
as if he were a hoopoe!° Why, he scared the old fig lady
so much she ran away and then he gobbled up the ripe ones.

COMMISSIONER
What will you women do to fix the mess we have in Greece?
How will you sort it out?

LYSISTRATA
               That's easy.

COMMISSIONER
                     How, though? Teach me.

LYSISTRATA (*taking the wool and spindle from the basket*)
                       Well,
when everything gets tangled up it's like a mess of wool.
We women hold our wool like *this* and wind strands of it
  deftly
around the spindle, some in this direction, some in that—
so, if allowed, we'll break this war down by untangling it
with envoys sent out, some in this direction, some in that.

COMMISSIONER
What, you think your spindles, wool and yarn can put an
  end   600
to so intractable a crisis? That's just stupid.

LYSISTRATA
                                          Yes,
That's what I think, and if you had a brain, you would conduct
all the affairs of Athens just as women handle wool.

COMMISSIONER
How? Make me understand.

LYSISTRATA
                    Imagine Athens is a fresh-shorn fleece.
First, what you do is dunk it in a bath and wash away
the sheep poop; then you lay it on a bed and take a stick
and beat out all the nasties, then you pick the thistles out.
Next, you take those that have stuck together and become
as thick as felt (to snag up all the civic offices)
and comb them out and pluck their heads off. Then you go
  and card   610
the raw cleaned wool into the Basket of Reciprocal
Agreeableness, mixing everyone in there together—
resident aliens and other foreigners you like
and those who owe the state back taxes—mix them in there
  good.
Next, you should think of all the cities that are colonies
of Athens as if they are scattered bits of wool. You take
these bits and bring them all together and combine them into
one big ball, from which you weave apparel for the people.

COMMISSIONER (*to the Chorus of Old Men*)
Isn't it crazy how these women prate about their sticks
and balls, while in the war they've never had a thing at
  stake?   620

LYSISTRATA

Nothing at stake? Prick, we have more than twice as much at
   stake
as you have! First off, we give birth to sons and send them out
to battle in your war—

COMMISSIONER

                         Shut up about that—don't remind me.

LYSISTRATA

Secondly, when we should be having good times and enjoying
being young, we have to sleep alone because our men
are on campaign. But let's forget about us wives—what hurts
is all the maidens growing old at home.

COMMISSIONER

                                   Don't men age, too?

LYSISTRATA

It's not the same. A man that comes back home can quickly
   find
some girl to marry, even if he is a graybeard geezer.
A woman has a briefer season. If she misses it,   630
no one will want to wed her. She will sit at home
   awaiting
marriage omens.

COMMISSIONER

              But whatever guy can still get hard—

LYSISTRATA

Drop dead. What's stopping you?
Here is your burial plot. Yes, you
may go and buy a coffin, sir,
and I will bake the honey cake
for Cerberus.°

(*giving the Commissioner a wreath*)

>Here, take my wreath.

FIRST OLD WOMAN (*giving the Commissioner ribbons*)
And I will give these ribbons to you.

SECOND OLD WOMAN (*giving the Commissioner another wreath*)
And here's another wreath from me.

LYSISTRATA
What else do you need? Embark.   640
Charon is calling out your name,°
and you are keeping him from sailing.

COMMISSIONER
Isn't the way they have been treating me
appalling? Yes, by Zeus, I'm going straight off
to show my fellow government officials
what has been done to me.

(*The Commissioner exits stage left with the four Scythian Archers.*)

LYSISTRATA
>You won't be lodging
complaints about the way we laid you out
for burial, will you? Well, I promise that,
two days from now, just after sunrise, we
will make the third-day offerings at your grave!°   650

(*Lysistrata exits into the Acropolis. The Three Old Women follow her, one of them carrying the basket of wool.*)

OLD MEN'S CHORUS LEADER
This is no time for sleeping. Every freeborn man should look
alive!

Let's strip, men, strip our jackets off to face this great emergency.

(*The Chorus of Old Men remove their jackets.*)

CHORUS OF OLD MEN
>   *Strophe*
>   My nose has just now caught
>   a whiff of something more significant.
>   Oh yes, there is the scent
>   of Hippias's tyranny° in this.
>   I greatly fear that certain Spartan men have met
>   at Cleisthenes's house°
>   and there agreed upon a plot
>   to stir up all the nasty women of   660
>   our town so that they seize the treasury
>   and by this action take away my life,
>   my means—my precious jury pay.

OLD MEN'S CHORUS LEADER
  It's terrible that they, mere women, now are criticizing fellow
  citizens and discussing bronze-wrought shields and, what is
     even worse,
     working to reconcile us with the Spartans, men less to be
       trusted
     than famished wolves! In actual fact the plot the women have
       been weaving
  is aimed at tyranny. But they will never tyrannize yours truly—
  I'll be prepared and henceforth "hide a sword inside a myrtle
     bough."
  I'll march in arms down to Aristogeiton's statue in the
     market°   670

(*striking a heroic pose*)

  and stand like *this* right next to him.

(*looking at the Old Women's Chorus Leader*)

>   Oh, how I've got an overwhelming
>   desire in me to sock this god-despised old woman on the jaw.

OLD WOMEN'S CHORUS LEADER

Try it, and your own mom won't recognize you when you get
  back home.
Rouse yourselves, fellow geriatrics! Lay your jackets on the
  ground.

(*The Chorus of Old Women remove their jackets.*)

CHORUS OF OLD WOMEN

> *Antistrophe*
> People, I shall begin
> by giving useful counsel to the state,
> and this is only right,
> seeing as it brought me up in noble splendor:
> at seven, I was Weaver of Athena's Gown;°
> at ten, I served as Grinder   680
> for Artemis the Foundress;° then,
> shedding my saffron robe, I danced as Bear
> at Brauron.° Next, a pretty maiden, back
> in Athens, I was Basket-Carrier
> and wore dried figs around my neck.°

OLD WOMEN'S CHORUS LEADER

That's why I owe good counsel to the state. Although I am a
  woman,
don't hold a grudge against me if I give far better counsel than
the nonsense we have now. I've got a stake in Athens: what I've
  paid
is men. You worthless fogeys haven't got a stake because you
  wasted
what you inherited, all that your fathers captured from the
  Persians,   690
and now you pay no taxes to replace it. We are almost
  ruined
because of you! Do you have anything to grumble in response?

(*The Chorus of Old Men make threatening gestures.*)

Upset me, and I'll use this rawhide boot to kick you in the jaw!

CHORUS OF OLD MEN

> *Strophe*
> Don't you think that womankind
> has finally gone too far?
> This mess is only getting worse from here.
> It's time for everyone with balls to make a
>   stand!

OLD MEN'S CHORUS LEADER

Strip your shirts off, since it's better when a man smells like
    a man.
We shouldn't be concealed inside our clothes like meat in
    ravioli.

(*The Chorus of Old Men remove their shirts.*)

CHORUS OF OLD MEN

> Come on, White Feet!° When we were in our
>   prime,   700
> we fought a tyrant at Leipsydrium.°
> We must rejuvenate ourselves. It's time
> to cast off this old skin
> so that our carcasses can fledge again.

OLD MEN'S CHORUS LEADER

If anybody on our side allows those hags the slightest
    handhold,
they will get their greedy mitts all over everything.
Sure, soon enough they will be building warships and, before we
    know it,
launching a fleet against us men like Artemisia.° If they turn
to horseback riding, you can cross out all our cavalry, because
women are made for mounting up and riding hard—you
    see, they never   710
slip out of the saddle! Take a look at Micon's paintings of
the Amazons°—see how they charge on horseback to attack
    the heroes.
We'd better grab these women by the necks and lock them in
    the stocks.

CHORUS OF OLD WOMEN
> *Antistrophe*
> Oh, but when I am on fire,
> I will attack you like
> a feral sow and send you bleating back
> home to your buddies with your hide clipped bare.

OLD WOMEN'S CHORUS LEADER (*to the Chorus of Old Women*)
  Quick, now, strip your outer layers off, so that we emanate
  the reek of women mad enough to use their teeth to bite their
    foes.

(*The Chorus of Old Women remove their clothing.*)

CHORUS OF OLD WOMEN
> If someone dares attack me, he will chew   720
> on no more garlic, no more beans. If you
> so much as toss curse words my way, I'll go
> crazy with rage and, like
> the beetle, make your eagle's eggs go "crack."°

OLD WOMEN'S CHORUS LEADER
  I won't be giving all you men another thought, not while
    Lampito
  and Ismenia, that distinguished Theban girl, are still alive.
  You have no power, not though you should pass the same law
    seven times.

(*to the Old Men's Chorus Leader*)

  You, jackass, are despised by everyone—all the Athenians
  and all your neighbors. Yesterday in fact, when I was
    celebrating
  Hecate with my friends,° I asked a fine and lovable girl
    over   730
  from just across the way—an eel out of Boeotia—but those
    neighbors

said that she couldn't come due to a law of yours. You'll go on
  passing
laws until someone grabs your leg and drags you off and breaks
  your neck!

(*The setting refocuses in time to several days later. The sex
strike has had its effect. Subsequently, all the male characters'
strapons are represented as erect. Lysistrata enters from a
stage door. She has a parchment in her pocket. For the opening eight lines of this scene the characters speak in a mock-
lofty pastiche.*)

Queen of our deed and plot, why dost thou enter
from out the palace with so dour a visage?

LYSISTRATA
Base women's actions and the female heart
cause me to pace about in deep despair.

OLD WOMEN'S CHORUS LEADER
What sayest thou? What sayest thou?

LYSISTRATA
'Tis true! 'Tis true!

OLD WOMEN'S CHORUS LEADER
Pray, what's the matter? Tell your confidantes.   740

LYSISTRATA
'Tis shame to speak, but cumbrous to conceal.

OLD WOMEN'S CHORUS LEADER
Do not conceal our miseries from me.

LYSISTRATA
Well, in a nutshell, then: we need a fuck.

OLD WOMEN'S CHORUS LEADER
O great Zeus!

LYSISTRATA
 Why call on Zeus? That's just the way things are.
 I've tried, but I can't keep them from their husbands
 any longer. They keep running off.
 The first one that I caught was over by
 Pan's Grotto,° digging out the hole; the second
 was trying to desert by sliding down   750
 a pulley rope. I caught another one
 just yesterday—she was astride a sparrow
 and hoped to fly to see Orsilochus.°
 I had to grab her by the hair. The women
 just keep on coming up with lame excuses
 to go back home.

(*The First Woman enters from the Acropolis.*)

                               Where are you running to?

FIRST WOMAN
 Home. I have fine Milesian wool there, wool
 that's being cut to bits by moths.

LYSISTRATA
                                What moths?
 Get back in there.

FIRST WOMAN
                     I'll go and come back quick.
 Just let me spread my wool out on the bed.   760

LYSISTRATA
 No spreading on the bed. No going home.

FIRST WOMAN
 So I just have to let my wool be wasted?

LYSISTRATA
 Yes, if necessary.

(*The Second Woman enters from the Acropolis.*)

SECOND WOMAN
                    Oh no, no,
my flax, I left my flax unscutched° at home.

LYSISTRATA
This other woman here is running off
to scutch her flax. You get right back inside.

SECOND WOMAN
I'll just go do some shucking and be back.

LYSISTRATA
No shucking! If I let you do your "shucking,"
the other girls will beg to do the same.

(*The Third Woman enters from the Acropolis. She has a helmet tucked under her shirt to simulate pregnancy.*)

THIRD WOMAN
Queen Eileithyia,° please delay my childbirth   770
until I get outside of sacred space.

LYSISTRATA
What are you saying?

THIRD WOMAN
                        I am giving birth!

LYSISTRATA
But you weren't even pregnant yesterday.

THIRD WOMAN
I am today. Oh, Lysistrata, let me go
home to my nurse as quick as I can run.

LYSISTRATA
What story are you making up?

(*knocking on the helmet*)

                              What hard
object are you concealing?

THIRD WOMAN
                          It's a boy!

LYSISTRATA
No, not a boy, but something hollow
and made of metal. Well, let's take a look.

(*Lysistrata removes the helmet from under the Third Woman's shirt.*)

What you are really saying is that you   780
are pregnant with Athena's Sacred Helmet.°

THIRD WOMAN
I'm pregnant, though. I swear to Zeus I am.

LYSISTRATA
Why did you have the helmet?

THIRD WOMAN
                          Well, I thought
that, if I started giving birth while still
up in Athena's temple, I could make
a sort of pigeon's nest out of the thing
and give birth there.

LYSISTRATA
                      What sort of lie is that?
A lame excuse. Your real intent is clear,
and you will have to stay up here until
your—helmet—has its name-day festival.   790

THIRD WOMAN
But I can't sleep on the Acropolis,
not since I saw the sacred guardian snake.

(*The Fourth Woman enters through a stage door.*)

FOURTH WOMAN

Oh, oh me! I am ruined utterly
because the owls keep going "who-who-who"
all night and I can't get to sleep!

LYSISTRATA

                          Enough
lies and excuses, girls. You're acting crazy!
No doubt you miss your men. But don't you think
that *they* miss *you*? You can be sure that they
are spending miserable nights. Good ladies,
be patient and endure a short while longer.   800
There is, in fact, an oracle foretelling
victory for us, if only we
do not become divided. Here it is.

(*Lysistrata takes out a parchment.*)

THIRD WOMAN

Go on and tell us what it says.

LYSISTRATA

                       Hush, now:
When all the swallows settle in a roost
separate from the hoopoes and desist
from congress with the feathered phalluses,
their problems will be solved. Loud-thundering Zeus
will turn all upside down—

THIRD WOMAN

                    And we will get
to ride on top?

LYSISTRATA

   ... *but if the swallows fight*   810
and fly out of the venerable shrine,
they will be seen as sluts by everyone.

THIRD WOMAN
  Well, that was blunt. Praise be to all the gods!

LYSISTRATA
  Though we are suffering, let's not surrender
  but go inside, dears. It would be a shame
  for us to act against the oracle.

(*Everyone exits into the Acropolis except the members of choruses.*)

CHORUS OF OLD MEN
  Strophe
  When I was a child
  I heard the story of a nice young man—
  Milanion.
  Running from marriage, he escaped into the
    wild   820
  and lived upon the mountain slopes,
  kept a dog, plaited rabbit traps,
  and never thought to go back home
  because he so detested *them*—
  the loathsome members of the female race.
  We hate them like he did, and we are wise.

OLD MEN'S CHORUS LEADER (*jokingly to the Women's Chorus Leader*)
      I want to kiss you, harridan—

OLD WOMEN'S CHORUS LEADER
      Stop eating onions, then.

(*The Old Men's Chorus Leader lifts his leg.*)

OLD MEN'S CHORUS LEADER
      . . . and raise my leg to kick you good.

OLD WOMEN'S CHORUS LEADER (*looking at the Old Men's Chorus Leader's crotch*)
      You've got a hairy sack indeed.   830

CHORUS OF OLD MEN
>General Myronides—
>he had a very shaggy crotch as well
>and flashed his black-haired butt-cheeks at his foes,
>and so did Phormion our admiral.

CHORUS OF OLD WOMEN
>*Antistrophe*
>I want to tell
>a tale to counter your "Milanion":
>There was a man,
>Timon, a wandering hermit hidden in a veil
>of stubborn thorns, the Furies' child.
>He also went into the wild   840
>and there tongue-lashed the whole male race.
>Yes, he despised you. Yes, like us,
>he thought you worthy of endless odium.
>But women—we were always dear to him.

OLD WOMEN'S CHORUS LEADER
>Want me to punch you in the jaw?

OLD MEN'S CHORUS LEADER (*sarcastically*)
>Oh no! You're scaring me!

OLD WOMEN'S CHORUS LEADER
>You want a kick? Would you like that?

OLD MEN'S CHORUS LEADER
>Do it, and you'll expose your twat.

OLD WOMEN'S CHORUS LEADER
>Well, if I do, you men
>won't see my pubes, old lady though I am,   850
>rough as a wilderness and overgrown.
>No, they are tidied by a candle's flame.

(*Lysistrata appears atop the wooden backdrop and spots a man
approaching from stage left.*)

LYSISTRATA
 Hip, hip, hooray! Come quick, now, ladies.

(*Myrrhine and the First Woman appear beside her, above.*)

FIRST WOMAN
                                                What's up?
 Tell us. What's all the hollering about?

LYSISTRATA
 A man, I see a crazed man coming, seized
 by orgiastic Aphrodite's powers.
 Goddess of Cyprus, Cythera and Paphos,
 the road you're coming down is very straight.

FIRST WOMAN
 Where is this mystery man?

LYSISTRATA
                            Beside the shrine
 of Chloe.

FIRST WOMAN
                Ah yes, now I make him out.   860
 Who is he, though?

LYSISTRATA
                Look closely, all of you.
 Does anybody recognize the man?

MYRRHINE
 Oh, that's my "better half"—my husband Harden.

LYSISTRATA
 Your mission is to spit him, roast him, turn him,
 to trick him, to adore and not adore him,
 to give him everything except those items
 the bowl that we have sworn by has forbidden.

MYRRHINE

No need to worry. I'll do what you ask.

LYSISTRATA

Still, I will stay close by to help you roast
and trick him. All you other women, go.

(*The First Woman and Myrrhine disappear from the top of the backdrop. Harden enters from stage left, wearing a disproportionately large, erect strap-on penis. With him is Manes the Slave carrying the Baby.*)

HARDEN

Oh, how I am afflicted! Cramps and spasms
torturing me like I'm on the rack!

LYSISTRATA

Who there has penetrated our defenses?

HARDEN

Me.

LYSISTRATA

A man?

HARDEN (*gesturing to his erection*)
            Yes, very much a man.

LYSISTRATA

Then very much get out of here.

HARDEN

                    And who
are you to drive me off?

LYSISTRATA

                Me, I'm the day watch.

HARDEN

Oh god! Just tell Myrrhine to come out here.

LYSISTRATA

What's with that "tell Myrrhine"? And who are you?

HARDEN

Her husband Harden, up from Dickersdale.°

LYSISTRATA

Hello, you darling. Yes, the name of "Harden"   880
is hardly seldom-heard and unrenowned
among us. You are always in your wife's mouth.
Always, when she eats an egg or apple,
she sighs, "If only this could be for Harden."

HARDEN (*suffering a spasm of pain*)

Damn, the pain!

LYSISTRATA

                    So help me, Aphrodite,
she says that. When we talk about our husbands,
she blurts out right away, "Compared with Harden,
all other husbands are just so much garbage."

HARDEN

Go on, then, call her out.

LYSISTRATA

                            What will you give me?

HARDEN (*gripping his erection*)

Well, if you want it, I've got this for you.   890
It's all the bribe I've got, but you can have it.

LYSISTRATA

Alright, I'll go and call Myrrhine.

(*Lysistrata disappears, above.*)

HARDEN

Just hurry!

(*to the audience*)

My life has had no pleasure in it, none,
since she has gone away. When I come home,
I only ache, and everything feels empty.
Not even food has any pleasure for me.
Damn, it's hard!

(*Myrrhine appears above.*)

MYRRHINE (*as if speaking to Lysistrata*)
I do adore him, yes,
adore him, but the man does not know how
to be adored. Don't make me go and meet him.

HARDEN

Myrrhie my sweet, why are you doing this?   900
Get down here, please!

MYRRHINE

I absolutely won't.

HARDEN

You won't come down here when I ask you to?

MYRRHINE

You ask, but you don't really, really need me.

HARDEN

Not need you? Life is agony without you.

MYRRHINE

I'm leaving.

HARDEN

Wait, wait—listen to the baby.

(*to the Baby*)

Hey, baby, call for Mama.

BABY

Mama! Mama!

HARDEN

What kind of mother are you? Six days now
your child has gone without a bath, unnursed,
and you feel nothing?

MYRRHINE

Oh, I feel for *him*.
His dad, though, doesn't give a damn about him.   910

HARDEN

You crazy girl, come down and see your baby!

MYRRHINE

What a thing it is to bear a child.
I must go down to him.

(*Myrrhine disappears from above.*)

HARDEN (*to the audience*)

What can I do?
Myrrhine seems so much younger than before.
Her glances have a sultry look, and all
her getting mad and flouncing back and forth
just makes me burn with passion even more.

(*Myrrhine enters from the Acropolis. She goes immediately to
the Baby.*)

MYRRHINE

O sweetie little baby! What a naughty
daddy you have. Let Mommy give you kisses.

HARDEN

Why are you acting like this, troublemaker?   920
Why are you listening to all those women?
You're killing me and injuring yourself.

(*Harden tries to drag Myrrhine off.*)

MYRRHINE (*resisting*)

Don't do it—don't you lay your hands on me.

HARDEN

But you are letting everything at home,
all of our possessions, go to ruin.

MYRRHINE

I really couldn't care at all about that.

HARDEN

It matters very little to you that
chickens are ripping up the tapestry
you had been working on?

MYRRHINE

Yes, very little.

HARDEN

For too long now the rites of Aphrodite   930
have gone uncelebrated by us. Please,
won't you come home?

MYRRHINE

I'll come back home as soon
as all you men make peace and end the war.

HARDEN

That's what we'll do . . . if we decide to do it.

MYRRHINE
I'll come home when you men decide to do it.
I've sworn an oath to stay right here till then.

HARDEN
Will you just lie down with me for a bit?
It's been so long.

MYRRHINE
           I won't. But I won't say
that I don't love you.

HARDEN
           Do you love me? Then
won't you lie down with me for just a little?   940

MYRRHINE
You joker. With the baby watching us?

HARDEN (*to Manes the Slave*)
Manes, take the baby home.

(*Manes takes the Baby off stage left.*)

(*to Myrrhine*)

           Alright,
the kid's no longer an impediment.
Won't you lie down?

MYRRHINE
           Where will we do it, though?

HARDEN
Pan's Grotto will be fine.

MYRRHINE
           How could I go
back up to the Acropolis, unbathed, impure,
after the act?

HARDEN
> No problem. Take a bath
in the Clepsydra.°

MYRRHINE
> Are you saying, love,
that I should break the oath I took?

HARDEN
> May all
the consequences light upon my head.
Don't think about the oath.

950

MYRRHINE
> Alright, but first
I need to go and get a bed.

HARDEN
> No way.
The ground will be just perfect for us.

MYRRHINE
> Never.
I'd never let you do it on the ground,
whatever sort of man you are.

(*Myrrhine goes offstage and returns with a cot.*)

HARDEN (*to the audience*)
> My wife
really does love me. Nothing could be clearer.

MYRRHINE
Here it is! You just take a load off there
and I will get undressed. But, darn, a mattress—
I should get a mattress.

HARDEN
> What, a mattress?
No need.

MYRRHINE
>   It would be awkward on the bed frame.   960

HARDEN
  Just kiss me.

MYRRHINE
>   Muh.

HARDEN
>   Damn, get that mattress quick!

(*Myrrhine goes offstage and returns with a mattress.*)

MYRRHINE
  Here it is! You just lie back down right there
  and I will get undressed. But, darn, a pillow—
  I should get a pillow.

HARDEN
>   I don't want one.

MYRRHINE
>   I do.

(*Myrrhine goes offstage.*)

HARDEN (*to the audience*)
  What, is my dick voracious Heracles
  forever waiting for his dinner now?°

(*Myrrhine returns with a pillow.*)

MYRRHINE
  Up, up. Sit up, now. Is that everything?

HARDEN
  Yes, everything. Come here, my precious one.

MYRRHINE
Yes, I'm just getting off my bra. Remember:
Don't let me down about the peace agreement.   970

HARDEN
Great Zeus, destroy me if I do.

MYRRHINE
                                Oh, but
you need a blanket.

HARDEN
                        I don't need a blanket—
I need a fuck!

MYRRHINE
                And, never fear, you'll get it—
right after I get back.

(*Myrrhine goes offstage.*)

HARDEN (*to the audience*)
                        The girl will drive me
crazy with all this bedclothes talk.

(*Myrrhine returns with a blanket.*)

MYRRHINE
                                Get up.

HARDEN
Oh, I am "up" already.

MYRRHINE
                        Want some scent?

HARDEN
God no.

MYRRHINE
>   By Aphrodite, I want scent,
> whether or not you want some.

HARDEN
>   Great Lord Zeus,
>   then pour it on.

(*Myrrhine goes offstage and returns with a flask of scent.*)

MYRRHINE
>   Hold out your hand and take some.
>   Rub yourself with it.

HARDEN
>   This is no sweet scent—   980
>   it feels like much delay and doesn't smell
>   like conjugal relations.

MYRRHINE
>   Oh, how silly,
>   I brought the scent from Rhodes.

HARDEN
>   It's good. Just leave it,
>   goofball.

MYRRHINE
>   What are you going on about?

(*Myrrhine goes offstage.*)

HARDEN (*to the audience*)
  My curses on the man who first made scent!

(*Myrrhine returns with another flask of scent.*)

MYRRHINE
  Here, use this flask.

HARDEN (*grabbing his erection*)
         I've got a big one here.
Lie down now, minx, and don't you go and get me anything
   more.

MYRRHINE
         Just as you say, and now
I'm taking off my shoes. Be sure, though, dearest,
to vote to make the peace.

(*Myrrhine silently exits through a stage door.*)

HARDEN
              I'll think about it.   990

(*realizing that Myrrhine has left*)

  She has destroyed me! Killed me! Even worse:
  she got me all worked up and then just left.

HARDEN
  Oh, what I'm going through! Where will I find a lover
  now that the fairest of them all has screwed me over?

(*gesturing to his erection*)

  How will I feed this offspring here? Where is the pimp
  Foxhound?° Let him come rent me out a nurse to pump.

OLD MEN'S CHORUS LEADER
    Terrible horrible pain
    must now be torturing your soul.
    I pity you, poor man—
    you have been played the fool.   1000

    What kidney could endure this much?
    What soul? What balls? What loins? What crotch
    strained like a victim on the rack?
    And, in the morning hours, no fuck!

HARDEN

O Zeus, the ache is back!

OLD MEN'S CHORUS LEADER

Your utterly revolting and appalling
wife has done these things to you.

HARDEN

No, she is gorgeous and enthralling.

OLD MEN'S CHORUS LEADER

No, by Zeus, she's wicked through and through.

HARDEN

Yes, by Zeus, she's wicked through and through.   1010

Zeus, send a firestorm or a great typhoon
to strike her like a little pile of grain
and set her spinning. Sweep her up, up, up,
then make her drop
back down toward earth again
and land precisely on my boner's tip.

(*A Spartan Messenger runs on from stage left. He is
wearing a disproportionately large, erect strap-on penis
hidden crudely beneath his robe. He speaks with a southern
twang.*)

SPARTAN MESSENGER

Where do y'all keep the Senate House in Athens?
Y'all's Assembly? I got news to tell.

HARDEN

What are you, then, a man or boner-monster?

SPARTAN MESSENGER

Me, I'm a messenger, ma boy, and I   1020
come here from Sparta to discuss a peace.

HARDEN
Is that a spear tucked up beneath your arm?

SPARTAN MESSENGER
I swear it ain't.

HARDEN
Why have you turned away?
Why tugged your cloak out there in front of you?
What, are your balls all swollen from the ride?

SPARTAN MESSENGER
You're crazy.

HARDEN
Dirty dawg, you've got a woody.

SPARTAN MESSENGER
Naw, naw, no woody. Cut out all your guff.

HARDEN
What do you call that thing?

SPARTAN MESSENGER
A Spartan staff.

HARDEN (*gesturing to his erection*)
Well, if it is, then here's my "Spartan staff."
Listen, I understand the situation.   1030
Now tell me truly: How are things in Sparta?

SPARTAN MESSENGER
Sparta is up in arms, and all her allies
are scared stiff. What we need's that whore Pellene!°

HARDEN
Who sent this plague upon you? Was it Pan?

SPARTAN MESSENGER

Naw, but Lampito was the one, I think.
Then all together, jus' like they were runners
leavin' a startin' gate, our other ladies
locked us menfolk outta their vaginas.

HARDEN

How are you holding up?

SPARTAN MESSENGER

        We got it, bad.
We hobble 'roun' the town a' Sparta doubled   1040
over like we luggin' lamps about.
Our ladies—they won't let us even touch
their nether cherries till we men agree
as one to make peace with the rest a' Greece.

HARDEN

So all the women everywhere in Greece
conspired to work this plot. I get it now.
Go back to Sparta quick as you can ride
and tell them there to send ambassadors
up here with absolute authority
to make a peace.

(*gesturing to his erection*)

        After presenting this—   1050
my cock—as evidence, I'll ask our council
to choose our own ambassadors as well.

SPARTAN MESSENGER

I'm flyin' off, now. What ya said's jus' right.

(*The Spartan Messenger exits stage left. Harden exits stage right.*)

OLD MEN'S CHORUS LEADER

Nothing, no, no animal, not even fire, is more unruly

than woman. Womankind is even more ferocious than a
  leopard.

OLD WOMEN'S CHORUS LEADER
  You admit all that but still insist on waging war on us.
  It's possible, you naughty boy, for us to have a lasting
    friendship.

OLD MEN'S CHORUS LEADER
  No, I never shall desist from loathing women. Never. NEVER!

OLD WOMEN'S CHORUS LEADER
  Whenever you are ready. Now, though, well—I just can't let
    you go
  around half-naked like that. Take a good look at yourself:
    you are   1060
  ridiculous. I'm coming over there to help you put your
    shirt on.

(*The Old Women's Chorus Leader helps the Old Men's Chorus
Leader put his shirt back on.*)

OLD MEN'S CHORUS LEADER
  Why, what you did for me just now was right, not wrong. I must
    admit
  that it was wrong of me to strip it off in rage a while ago.

OLD WOMEN'S CHORUS LEADER
  The first thing is that you look like a man again; the second
    thing,
  that you no longer look ridiculous. If you weren't such a grump,
  I'd have removed that insect from your eye for you. It's still there
    now.

OLD MEN'S CHORUS LEADER
  So that's what has been irritating me! You take this little ring
  and plow the thing out of my eye. Then, when you're done, please
    show it to me.
  By Zeus, that insect has been gnawing on my eye for ages now!

OLD WOMEN'S CHORUS LEADER
  Alright, I'll do it for you. Just you don't be such a
    grumpy-face.   1070

(*The Old Women's Chorus Leader takes the ring and uses it
to remove the mosquito from the Old Men's Chorus Leader's
eye.*)

  By Zeus, what a gargantuan mosquito you had in your eye!
  Just look at this! A monster spawned within the swamps of
    Tricorysia!°

OLD MEN'S CHORUS LEADER
  Thanks very much. That monster had been digging pits in me
    for days.
  Now that you've gotten rid of my mosquito, I can't keep from
    weeping.

OLD WOMEN'S CHORUS LEADER
  Though you are quite a naughty boy, I'll wipe your tears away . . .
    and kiss you.

OLD MEN'S CHORUS LEADER
  No kissing!

OLD WOMEN'S CHORUS LEADER
  I am going to kiss you whether you consent or not.

OLD MEN'S CHORUS LEADER
  I wish you all bad luck.

(*The Old Women's Chorus Leader kisses the Old Men's Chorus
Leader.*)

  You women were just born to be persuasive.
  There is a proverb that has got the thing just right: we men
    can live
  neither *with* nor *without* all you wretches. All the same, I now

declare a peace: henceforth we'll never do you wrong, and,
   you all, never   1080
do us wrong as well. Let's join together and begin our song:

(*The Old Men's Chorus Leader and the Old Women's Chorus
Leader unite.*)

CHORUS
    Strophe
    Gentlemen, we're not here to make a scandal of
    some citizen's behavior. No, instead,
    we only want to say and do what's good.
    Your present troubles are already quite enough.

    Let every man and wife
    who need a little money—say,
    a whole year's salary—
    come ask us for a loan.
    We've got that sum at home and bags to put it in.   1090
    And, if we ever get to live at peace again,
    our debtors need not pay us back—
    because they won't have gotten jack!

    Antistrophe
    This evening we will entertain distinguished,
      gracious
    gentlemen from Carystus.° We have soup.
    We have a suckling pig, which I cut up
    for sacrifice. (I kept the choice and juiciest pieces.)

    Come over to my house this
    evening. Be sure to take a bath,
    but come on over with   1100
    your wife and kids in tow.
    Trust me, you won't need anyone's permission—no,
    just walk on up as if the place belonged to you.
    What will be waiting for you there?
    A stiffly locked and bolted door!

(*Two Spartan Ambassadors enter from stage left. They are
wearing disproportionately large, erect strap-on penises
beneath their cloaks. They speak with a southern twang.*)

CHORUS LEADER
  Here come the Spartan Ambassadors—bearded
  gentlemen wearing something like wicker
  pig-cages strapped between their thighs.

  First off: my greetings to you, men of Sparta.
  Second: please tell me how you have been doing.   1110

SPARTAN AMBASSADOR
  Heck, what's the use a' gabbin' on and on:
  Y'all can see quite clear jus' how we're doin'.

(*The Spartan Ambassadors remove their cloaks, exposing
their erections.*)

CHORUS LEADER
  Goodness, what awful diplomatic tension.
  This mess was hot but now looks even hotter.

SPARTAN AMBASSADOR
  Words jus' can't say it. Let some fella come
  and make a treaty any way he fancies.

(*Two Athenian Ambassadors enter from stage right. They,
too, are wearing disproportionately large, erect strap-on
penises.*)

CHORUS LEADER
  And now I see these native sons of Athens
  letting the robes hang forward from their stomachs
  like wrestlers crouching for a hold. It looks
  like they have got some bad groin injuries.   1120

ATHENIAN AMBASSADOR
  We'd like to know where Lysistrata is.
  We men are here, as you can clearly see.

CHORUS LEADER
  These men's afflictions match up with the others.'
  The spasms—do they strike worst late at night?

ATHENIAN AMBASSADOR
  Yes, and we can't stop getting chafed down there.
  If someone doesn't reconcile us soon,
  we'll all be forced to go fuck Cleisthenes.

CHORUS LEADER
  Be careful, now, and cover up or else
  someone will come and mutilate your . . . Herms.°

ATHENIAN AMBASSADOR
  Thank you. That is excellent advice.   1130

SPARTAN AMBASSADOR
  Sure is. Come on, let's put our cloaks back on.

(*The Ambassadors all cover up their erections with their cloaks.*)

ATHENIAN AMBASSADOR (*to the Spartan Ambassadors*)
  Spartans, hello. We've suffered quite a bit.

SPARTAN AMBASSADOR
  Buddy, we're sufferin' something fierce as well.

(*gesturing to the audience*)

  I hope them choppers a' the Herms don't see us!

ATHENIAN AMBASSADOR
  Spartans, let's get down to the nitty-gritty.
  Why have you come here?

SPARTAN AMBASSADOR
                              As ambassadors
   to make a peace.

ATHENIAN AMBASSADOR
                         Great news. That's why we're here
   as well. Why don't we call in Lysistrata?
   She's the one to bring us all together.

SPARTAN AMBASSADOR
   Heck, if you like, go call her brother, too.   1140

(*Lysistrata enters from the Acropolis.*)

ATHENIAN AMBASSADOR
   Why, there's no need to call her—here she is.
   She must have heard us when we said her name.

CHORUS LEADER (*to Lysistrata*)
   Greetings to you, most manly of women.
   It's time for you to be clever and gentle,
   classy and trashy, severe and sweet—
   in sum, a universal lady.
   Seduced by the power of your amorous magic,
   important men have gathered together
   from all over Greece to lay their many
   disputes before your arbitration.   1150

LYSISTRATA (*to the Chorus Leader*)
   They're not so hard to manage if you catch them
   when they are aroused and not attacking
   one another. Well, we'll find out soon.
   Where is Reconciliation?

(*Reconciliation, a voluptuous female, enters, nude, from a stage door.*)

(*to Reconciliation*)

Go

and bring those Spartans over here by me.
Do not be rough or overbearing with them
or paw them boorishly the way our husbands
have handled us, but touch them like a woman—
domestically. If he won't offer up
his hand, you'll have to grab him by the dick.   1160
Now go get those Athenians as well.
Take hold of what they offer up and drag them over here.

(*to the Spartans and Athenians*)

You Spartans, stand right here
beside me; you Athenians, right here.
Now listen to my words: I am a woman,
yes, but I have a brain. Although I've got
plenty of intellect in my own right,
I've also listened frequently to what
my father and his friends were talking over,
so I've become quite educated, too.   1170
Now that I have you here, I want to scold you,
both sides, in common, as is only just.

Both Spartans and Athenians, like kinsmen,
sprinkle the altars from a single bowl
of sacred water at Olympia,
at Pytho, at Thermopylae°—how many
other places could I add to make
the list still longer? But, though there are foreign
enemies out there with their armies, you
wage war against Greek men and towns in Greece.   1180
One point, my first, has now been driven home.

ATHENIAN AMBASSADOR
My dick's about to burst out of its skin!

LYSISTRATA (*to the Spartans*)
Next, Spartans, I will turn my words on you.
Have you forgot how Pericleidas° came
and, though a Spartan, took a seat upon

a shrine in Athens as a suppliant,
a pale man in a vivid red cloak, begging
for military aid? Your subject state
Messenia had attacked you, and Poseidon
had shocked you with a quake. Our Cimon took   1190
four thousand infantry and saved all Sparta.
Since you have received such benefits
from the Athenians, why do you Spartans
ravage the land that gave you so much aid?

ATHENIAN AMBASSADOR
They've done us an injustice, Lysistrata!

SPARTAN AMBASSADOR
We sure did.

(*looking at Reconciliation's behind*)

        Dang, she's got a luscious ass.

LYSISTRATA (*to the Athenians*)
Now, don't assume that I'll be letting you
Athenians off scot-free. Don't you remember,
when you were dressed in sheepskin clothes like slaves,
how Spartans showed up with their spears and killed   1200
many Thessalian men and many allies
and friends of Hippias as well?° That day
they were the only ones who helped you kick
the tyrant out. Don't you remember how
they came and liberated you and how
they wrapped your people in a cloak again?

SPARTAN AMBASSADOR (*gawking at Reconciliation*)
Me, I never seen a nicer woman.

ATHENIAN AMBASSADOR (*looking at Reconciliation's crotch*)
And me, I've never seen a finer pussy.

LYSISTRATA
You've done so many favors for each other.
Why are you fighting? Why not put an end   1210
to all this turmoil? Why not make a peace?
Come on, what's stopping you?

SPARTAN AMBASSADOR (*looking at Reconciliation's buttocks*)
                                        We come 'roun' to't, if one
a' y'all come 'roun' to giving us this here
round mountain on her backside.

ATHENIAN AMBASSADOR
                                        What round mountain?

SPARTAN AMBASSADOR
Why, Pylos, that's the thing that we been gropin'
and hankerin' after for a long time now.

ATHENIAN AMBASSADOR
No, by Poseidon, you will not get Pylos!°

LYSISTRATA (*to the Athenian Ambassador*)
Be a good man, now, and give it to them.

ATHENIAN AMBASSADOR
Where will we go to get some loving, then?

LYSISTRATA
Just ask for somewhere else as compensation.   1220

ATHENIAN AMBASSADOR (*looking at Reconciliation's front*)
Alright, then. Give us this, er, mound right here,
Echinous, and the Malian Gulf behind it,
and both these long legs stretching out of Megara.°

SPARTAN AMBASSADOR
Dang, we ain't gonna give y'all everythin'!

LYSISTRATA (*to the Athenian Ambassador*)
Just let it drop. Why wrangle over legs?

ATHENIAN AMBASSADOR (*looking at Reconciliation's crotch*)
I want to strip right now and start my plowing!

SPARTAN AMBASSADOR (*looking at Reconciliation's buttocks*)
I'll git up with the sun and spread manure!

LYSISTRATA
After you both have sworn to the agreement,
you each can get down to your business. Now,
if it seems best to you to make this peace,   1230
go and present your allies with the terms.

ATHENIAN AMBASSADOR
Allies, my dear? Just look how hard I am.
Won't all our allies reach the same decision—
to fuck?

SPARTAN AMBASSADOR
      Our allies sure will do the like.

ATHENIAN AMBASSADOR
Our Carystian men—they'll go along.

LYSISTRATA
Alright, then. You must purify yourselves
so that my girls and I can entertain you
on the Acropolis and share with you
the food we have inside our wicker baskets.
There you will conclude the peace with oaths   1240
on both sides. Then you all may claim your wives
and go back home.

ATHENIAN AMBASSADOR
                    Well, let's get going, then.

SPARTAN AMBASSADOR
  Y'all fetch me where I need to go.

ATHENIAN AMBASSADOR
                              And quickly!

(*Everyone exits into the Acropolis except the members of the
Chorus.*)

CHORUS
          Strophe
          Embroidered tapestries, nice clothing, fancy gowns,
          even my gold, all this—I willingly provide
          to everybody to supply their sons
          or dress their daughters for the Big Parade.
          I welcome you to come and take
          everything that I have in stock.
          Nothing is sealed up so well   1250
          that you can't break the seal
          and take whatever you might find inside.
          Ah, but unless you're blessed with better eyes than me,
          there won't be anything to see.

          Antistrophe
          If anyone is out of bread and has a lot
          of slaves to feed and lots of little children, too,
          come borrow flour from me—small grains of it,
          but, taken all together, they would grow
          into a healthy-looking loaf.
          And all you who are paupers, if   1260
          you bring your own bags to my house,
          my servant boy Manes
          will pour in little grains of flour for you.
          Be careful, though: if ever you come to my door,
          you'll find a killer watchdog there.

(*The Athenian Ambassador emerges with another Athenian from a stage door. They are very drunk. The first Athenian Ambassador is carrying a torch. A Doorkeeper and several Slaves are sitting on the ground near the door.*)

ATHENIAN AMBASSADOR (*to the Doorkeeper*)
  Open the door there, you. You should have moved.

(*to the Slaves*)

  You slaves, what are you doing sitting there?
  Yeah, maybe I should burn you with this torch.
  That's shtick, though. I would never do it.

(*addressing the audience*)

                                         Well,
  if you *insist* I do it, then I'll go
  all-out and do the audience a favor.   1270

(*He chases the Slaves off with the torch.*)

ATHENIAN (*helping to chase the Slaves off*)
  Me, too. I'll go all-out along with you.

(*to the Slaves*)

  Git, now! I'll burn your hair until you scream.

ATHENIAN AMBASSADOR
  Yeah, git, so that the Spartans, when they come out
  after the feast, enjoy some peace and quiet.

ATHENIAN (*to the Athenian Ambassador*)
  I've never seen a party so fantastic!
  The Spartans, for their part, were charming guests,
  and we were pretty clever in our cups.

ATHENIAN AMBASSADOR
  That's what I would expect, since, when we're sober,
  we go astray. If the Athenians   1280

would only listen to me, we would always
go on ambassadorial missions drunk.
As things are now, when we arrive in Sparta
sober, we look for ways to cause a ruckus;
and we don't hear whatever they are saying
and, when they don't say boo, we turn suspicious.
So we wind up with rival versions of
the same events. But everything was perfect
this time around. When someone started singing
the *Telamon*, when he should have been singing   1290
Cleitagora,° we all just whooped and swore
that there was no mistake.

(*The Slaves return and sit down again.*)

                    Those slaves have all
come back again. Get out of here, you vagrants!

(*He chases the Slaves off with the torch again.*)

ATHENIAN
Here are the Spartans right now, coming out.

(*The Spartan Ambassador emerges with other Spartans and a
Piper.*)

SPARTAN AMBASSADOR
Hey, piper, grab your flute, now, 'cause I'm gonna
dance a two-step while I sing a pretty
Spartan ditty for the men a' Athens.

ATHENIAN AMBASSADOR
Piper, by all the gods, take up your flute.
I just love watching Spartans do their dances.

SPARTAN AMBASSADOR (*singing while he dances*)
  O Goddess a' Rememberin', rouse   1300
  for me a Muse who knows
  all a' the Spartans' and Athenians' deeds—
  how, off the Cape a' Artemisium,

the men a' Athens spread their sails like gods
and beat the navy a' the Medes,
while Spartans under Leonidas fought on land°
like boars. Like boars, we gnashed our tusks, and foam
ran from our jaws, and sweat ran down our thighs.
The Persian troops outnumbered grains a' sand
upon the shore.

                     O Goddess a' the Wilderness,   1310
Beast-Slayer Virgin Power, come
join in this treaty, help us live
in harmony a good long time.
Let lots a' amity attend
always this sacred peace.
Let us forever put a' end
to foxy guile and stratagem.
O Virgin Huntress, come here, please.

ATHENIAN AMBASSADOR
Well, now that everything has come together,
you Spartans may reclaim your spouses here.   1320
Let every husband stand beside his woman,
and every woman by her man. Let's hold a dance
in honor of the gods to celebrate
today's successes, and let's promise never,
ever again, to make the same old blunders.

CHORUS
Begin the dancing, bring the Graces in
and Artemis and her dance-leading twin,
Apollo, the kindhearted healing power,
and Dionysus with his eyes aflame,
guiding the madwomen who follow him,   1330
and King Zeus brandishing his bolts of fire
and Hera, prosperous wife of Zeus,
and many other deities
to serve as witnesses
of the magnanimous Peace
that Aphrodite made for us.

Hip, hip, hooray!
Hooray, it's like a victory!
Lift your legs up high.
Hip, hip, hooray!   1340

ATHENIAN AMBASSADOR
My Spartan friend, since we have sung a new song,
share a new song of your own with us.

SPARTAN AMBASSADOR (*singing while he dances*)
Come, Spartan Muse, from handsome Tayeegety
and celebrate this friendship with a ditty
in honor a' the gods
Apollo and Athena a' the Brazen House°
and both the sons a' King Tyndareus
riding their steeds
beside the Eurotas.°

Come on and leap,   1350
now! Up, now, up!
Let's sing in praise a' Sparta where
everyone in the sacred choir
sings, and the sound of dancing gives
off echoes, where the girls like fillies raise
dust clouds while running with the Eurotas,
where they have great fun, waving sacred staves
under the tutelage a' Leda's daughter,°
their fine and pious chorus leader.

(*to the Chorus*)

Come, now, and tie your hair up with a ribbon. Like a deer
   now, leap,   1360
and make a brouhaha to keep the people dancin', while
   you sing
in honor a' invincible Athena a' the Brazen House.

(*The ensemble dances together and then exits stage left and
right.*)

Notes

2–3 *the Goddesses of Sex / at Colias*: Lysistrata feels that if the women had been called to celebrate a raucous religious festival, they would already be present. The three festivals she lists as examples are in honor of Dionysus (Bacchus), Pan, and, lastly, the Genetyllides (Goddesses of Sex, including Aphrodite) at a temple on a cape "Colias," the location of which is unknown.

39 *their precious eels*: The eels of Lake Copais in Boeotia were regarded as a great delicacy in Athens.

54 *by Demeter and Persephone*: Calonice swears a mild oath by the two goddesses Demeter and Kore (Persephone). This is a specifically woman's oath.

61 *always later than they should be*: Athenians were stereotypically tardy.

63 *over from Salamis and the Paralia*: Salamis is a large island in the Saronic Gulf, and the Paralia is coastal Attica. These seafaring sections of greater Athens serve as a feed for the subsequent double entendre about females "riding" on a boat/having sex mounted on the male.

65 *the Acharnian women*: The Acharnians (people of the deme Acharnae) were supposedly especially anti-Spartan. Their lands had suffered great destruction as a consequence of the Spartan incursions into Attica during the Peloponnesian War.

67–68 *Theogenes's wife . . . high to get here*: Mention of Acharnae prompts a joke about the wife of presumably Acharnian Theogenes. Theogenes was a fairly common name, and it is impossible to pin down a historical figure. The joke seems to be that Theogenes's wife is a drunk, as there is a double entendre on *akateion* (sail/wine cup) in the original.

71 *Stinkydale*: "Stinkydale" translates the geographical region of Anagyrous, a swampy region named for the malodorous plant *anagyros*.

107–108 *in Thrace fighting to save Eucrates / the general*: Thrace (now split between Bulgaria, Greece, and Turkey) was strategically important to the Athenians throughout the Peloponnesian War. Nothing more is known about this general Eucrates.

109 *Pylos*: The Athenians had captured (in 425 B.C.E.) and still held (in 411 B.C.E.) the peninsula of Pylos at the southwestern end of the Peloponnesus.

115 *those five-inch dildos*: The Ionian city of Miletus had defected to the Spartan side in 412 B.C.E. As Miletus was the major producer of dildos, the Athenians would have had difficulty importing them.

125 *Mount Tayeegety*: Mount Taygetus (southwest of Sparta) is, at 7,887 feet, the tallest mountain in Laconia.

147 *hump and dump*: The original reads, in translation, "Poseidon and a tub." The tragedian Sophocles twice portrayed Poseidon's seduction of Tyro and her subsequent exposure of their twin sons in a tub beside a river.

166 *lickety-split he threw his sword aside*: In myth, Menelaus, though he intends to kill Helen of Troy, drops his sword when she exposes her breasts to him.

168–169 *Well, like a poet . . . dildo away*: The "poet" referred to here is the comic playwright Pherecrates, an older contemporary of Aristophanes. The joke turns on the fact that dildos were often covered in dog skin.

187 *and tons a' money in Athena's temple*: The treasuries of Athena on the Acropolis were Athens's main financial reserve in 411 B.C.E.

189–190 *to occupy the hilltop fortress / of the Acropolis this very morning*: Lysistrata reveals that she has sent another group of women to seize the Acropolis (and thus secure the treasury for the Delian League and the treasuries of Athena).

207 *they slit a victim's throat above a shield*: Lysistrata here mentions a scene in Aeschylus's tragedy *Seven Against Thebes*, first produced in 469 B.C.E. In it seven allied leaders swear an oath with their hands dipped in the blood of a horse.

210–211 *What if we got / a pure-white steed somewhere and cut it up?*: Horse sacrifice is highly exceptional in ancient Greek culture. Calonice's proposal is ridiculous.

216 *never to add a drop of water*: The ancient Greeks controlled the potency of wine by "cutting" it with a greater or lesser amount of water. The joke here is that the women will drink wine from the island of Thasos, a particularly dark and aromatic wine, uncut.

276 *Draces*: Aristophanes includes names of members of both choruses. I have retained the names only of Draces for the men's chorus leader and Stratyllis for the women's chorus leader.

289 *Lycon's drunken wife*: Lycon's wife had a reputation for promiscuous behavior. The old men here suspect that she has instigated the female uprising.

291 *Cleomenes*: In 508 B.C.E., the Spartan general Cleomenes came to Athens with Spartan troops at the invitation of the Athenian Isagoras and seized the Acropolis. His intention was to help Isagoras establish in Athens an oligarchic government sympathetic to Sparta. After a two-day occupation of the Acropolis, he was allowed to depart with troops as part of a truce. These lines are humorous because of the hyperbole—they claim that they received the spear of Cleomenes (even though his surrender took place ninety-seven years prior to 411 B.C.E.), in which case they would be well over a hundred years old. They also exaggerate the two-day occupation to "six years."

300 *Euripides as well*: In fifth-century comedy, Euripides is famous for misogyny.

301 *May Marathon no longer feature my memorial*: The chorus members claim to have been *Marathonomachoi* (veterans of the Battle of Marathon). In 490 B.C.E. a vastly outnumbered army consisting of Athenians and Plataeans defeated the Persian army camped at Marathon in southeast Attica. A monument at the battle site commemorated the victory.

312 *Great Lord Heracles!*: An oath uttered by males to express shock. Heracles is appropriate in relation to fire in that he immolates himself on Mount Oeta.

315 *the Lemnian sort of fire*: The island of Lemnos is associated with fire because of the volcano on it. Here there is an untranslatable pun on Lemnos and the word *lēmē* ("eyesore" or "mote in the eye").

328–329 *generals at the naval base / in Samos, do you want to help us stack this lumber?*: Samos was the Athenian naval headquarters for northern Greece, with seventy-three ships. The old men of the chorus, elsewhere self-identified as proud infantrymen, ask whether the members of the navy might want to help them drive the women off the Acropolis.

332 *Victory Goddess Nike*: Nike, goddess of victory, is in the retinue of Athena, goddess of wisdom and warcraft. It is likely that the men are represented as praying to Nike in her temple on a bastion overlooking the Propylaea of the Acropolis.

361 *Golden-Crested Fortress Guardian*: "Golden-Crested" refers to the tiara worn by the image of Athena Polias in the Parthenon. Among Athena's prerogatives was the protection of hilltop fortresses in general and of the Acropolis in Athens in particular.

363 *Tritogeneia*: This epithet for Athena first appears in Hesiod and is commonly interpreted as referring to her birthplace in Lake Tritonis in Libya. *Iambi et Elegi Graeci: Ante Alexandrum Cantati*, Vol I: Archilochus, Hipponax Theognidea, ed. Martin L. West (Oxford, UK: Oxford University Press), 2nd ed. 1989.

377 *Bupe-Bupe-Bupalus*: The sixth-century poet of invective Hipponax threatens to punch his enemy, Bupalus, in fragment 120 West: "Take my cloak, I'll hit Bupalus in the eye! For I have two right hands and I don't miss with my punches" (translated by Douglas Gerber). According to one ancient source, Hipponax so viciously attacked Bupalus with invective verse that Bupalus hanged himself (Pseudo-Acron on Horace, *Epodes*, cited by Douglas Gerber in *Greek Iambic Poetry*, Loeb Classical Library No. 259 [Cambridge, MA: Harvard University Press, 1999], 351).

396 *You aren't on a jury now!*: Older men in Athens tended to make an income by serving on juries.

405 *that exotic god Sabezius*: Sabezius was an ecstatic Phrygian deity who arrived in Athens in the 430s B.C.E. As his worship involved drinking to excess, he was associated with Dionysus.

406 *Adonis*: The worship of Adonis in Greece, similar to that of Dumuzi (Tammuz) in Egypt, was exclusive to women and involved ritual lamentation over the annual death of Adonis and the cultivation of "Adonis gardens" on rooftops.

413 *Zacynthus*: The Commissioner is recounting speeches given by the politician Demostratus in the months leading up to the disastrous Sicilian expedition, which began in 415 B.C.E. Demostratus pushed both for the expedition and for the recruitment of hoplites (foot soldiers) from the island of Zacynthus.

424 *By Poseidon*: The Commissioner aptly swears a mild oath by Poseidon, god of the sea, in response to the chorus's complaint of being drenched.

468 *a cup*: The Second Old Woman refers to the practice of "cupping" a black eye. Cupping therapy, now classified as a pseudoscience, was and is believed to have positive effects such as pain relief and wrinkle reduction.

485 *Don't wait to strip the corpses*: In the *Iliad*, Homeric heroes customarily stripped the armor from the soldiers they had killed.

548 *War is an affair for men*: The Trojan hero Hector utters these words in Homer's *Iliad* (6.492).

564–565 *get some beans / to chew on*: Both male and female Athenians chewed beans while doing repetitive tasks.

591 *a hoopoe*: "Hoopoe" translates the Thracian hero Tereus, who was transformed into a hoopoe after raping his wife Procne's sister Philomel; see Ovid, *Metamorphoses* 6.671ff.

636–637 *the honey cake / for Cerberus*: The dead presumably used honey cakes to placate wardens of the underworld, such as Cerberus, in much the same way that visitors to underground shrines used them to placate sacred snakes.

641 *Charon is calling out your name*: Charon, the ferryman of the underworld, is here represented as summoning the "dead" Commissioner to embark and cross the river Styx.

650 *the third-day offerings at your grave*: Counting from either the *prosthesis* (setting forth of the body for viewing) or burial, offerings were given to the dead on the third, ninth, and thirteenth days and annually thereafter.

656 *Hippias's tyranny*: Hippias, the last tyrant of Athens, was driven out in 510 B.C.E.

658 *Cleisthenes' house*: Frequently mocked as an effeminate in the plays of Aristophanes, Cleisthenes is here accused of being sympathetic to the Spartans as well.

670 *Aristogeiton's statue in the market*: In 514 B.C.E. two Athenians, Harmodius and Aristogeiton, assassinated Hipparchus, the brother of the tyrant Hippias. They were subsequently regarded as heroes of the democracy, and statues of them were set up in the *agora* (marketplace) of Athens.

679 *Weaver of Athena's Gown*: The chorus members cite their service in various female religious roles as evidence of their patriotism. First, at the age of seven, they served as *arrhephoroi*, weavers of the sacred *peplos* for the statue of Athena Polias.

681 *Artemis the Foundress*: Second, they served as grain-grinders for the sacred cakes of Artemis the Foundress.

682–683 *Bear / at Brauron*: Third, they served as *arktoi*, she-bears, in the Brauronia, a festival held every five years, in which girls performed ritual dances dressed as bears.

684–685 *Basket-Carrier / and wore dried figs around my neck*: Finally, when they were of marriageable age, females could serve as *kanephoroi* (basket-carriers) for the annual Panathenaea festival in Athens. Dried figs are associated with sexuality and fertility.

700 *"White Feet"*: "White Feet" is most likely an honorific address to foot soldiers.

701 *Leipsydrium*: In 514 B.C.E. the family of the Alcmaeonidae and other exiles from Athens fortified the city of Leipsydrium on a slope of Mount Parnes near Athens in a failed attempt to procure their re-enfranchisement in the state; see Herodotus, *Histories* 5.62.

708 *Artemisia*: Artemisia, queen of Caria, fought on the side of Xerxes and the Persians in the naval battle of Salamis, 480 B.C.E.; see Herodotus, *Histories* 7.99, 8.87–88.

711–712 *Micon's paintings of / the Amazons*: Amazons, warrior women, were believed to have invaded the area around the Acropolis in mythic times. In the middle of the fifth century B.C.E. Micon painted an "Amazonomachy" (a battle between Theseus and the Amazons) in the Stoa Poikile to accompany other paintings by his teacher Polygnotus.

723–724 *like / the beetle . . . "crack"*: The Chorus of Old Women alludes here to Fable 3 of Aesop, in which a beetle, in retaliation for a wrong done to it, breaks an eagle's eggs. The women are threatening, figuratively, to injure the men's testicles.

729–730 *when I was celebrating / Hecate with my friends*: Hecate is a popular deity, especially for women. For the eel of Lake Copais as a delicacy, see note above, line 39.

749 *Pan's Grotto*: This cave is located on the north face of the Acropolis in Athens.

753 *Orsilochus*: In addition to being associated with Aphrodite, the *strouthos* (sparrow) was a slang term for penis. Although this Orsilochus is unknown, the context suggests he was a gigolo or pimp.

764 *unscutched*: "Scutching" is the process by which impurities are removed from raw material. The Second Woman is referring to separating the straw and stems from flax.

770 *Queen Eileithyia*: Daughter of Zeus and Hera, Eileithyia is the goddess of childbirth, usually sent at Hera's behest. Giving birth, a ritually impure activity, was not permitted on hallowed ground.

781 *Sacred Helmet*: The cult image of Athena Parthenos wore a helmet that featured a sphinx flanked by two griffons.

879 *Harden, up from Dickersdale*: I have opted to translate the name Cinesias here as "Harden" to distinguish this character from the dithyrambic poet Cinesias who appears in *Birds*. The scholar Jeffrey Henderson hears a pun on Cinesias (*kinein*, "to fuck") and on the deme Paeonides (*paiein*, "to bang").

948 *the Clepsydra*: After sex, one could become ritually pure (so as to enter sacred space) by bathing in flowing water. The Clepsydra was a spring on the western side of the Acropolis.

965–967 *is my dick . . . his dinner now?*: In comedy Heracles is often portrayed as a glutton who is being cheated out of a feast.

996 *Foxhound*: "Foxhound" is the nickname of the pimp Philostratus; see Aristophanes's *Knights*, 1089.

1033 *Pellene*: The most easterly of the cities of mountainous Achaea, Pellene was on the coastal strip of Arcadia. The Spartan Messenger here talks about the city as if it were a female.

1072 *the swamps of Tricorysia*: Tricorysia was a forested, swampy area on the eastern coast of Attica. One could imagine insects growing to an impressive size there.

1095 *Carystus*: Carystus, an ally, had troops stationed in Athens.

1129 *mutilate your . . . Herms*: Herms were boundary-marking statues featuring a head of Hermes and an erect phallus. In 415 B.C.E., before the Sicilian expedition departed, Herms were famously "mutilated" (disfigured), allegedly by the aristocrat Alcibiades and his friends.

1175–1176 *at Olympia / at Pytho, at Thermopylae*: Lysistrata refers to several Panhellenic athletic sites in the Greek-speaking world: the Olympian and the Pythian games, and the Pylaea at Thermopylae. Competitors traveled to and participated in these games under the protection of a sacred truce, even during wartime.

1184 *Pericleidas*: In 464 B.C.E. there was a major earthquake in Laconia. The helots, or serf population, there revolted. Pericleidas, a king of the Spartans, came to Athens and asked for assistance in suppressing the uprising. In response to his request, Cimon, an Athenian general, led four thousand Athenian troops to assist the Spartans.

1200–1202 *Spartans showed up . . . Hippias as well*: In 510 B.C.E. Cleomenes the Spartan king led his troops against Hippias, the tyrant of Athens, his supporters, and his Thessalian cavalry and drove them out of the city.

1217 *Pylos*: See note above, line 109.

1221–1223 *this, er, mound . . . out of Megara*: Geography represents anatomy here through double entendre. Echinous refers, on a literal level, to a city in Phthiotis (northern Greece) held by the Spartans since 426 B.C.E., and the Malian Gulf is the coastline in Phthiotis, in the western Aegean Sea. The scholar Jeffrey Henderson argues that they refer, through double entendre, to pubic hair and the vulva, respectively. *both these long legs* refers to the long walls connecting the city of Megara to its port, Nisaea.

1289–1291 *singing / the* Telamon *. . . been singing /* Cleitagora: The *Telamon* and *Cleitagora* are both *skolia*, songs written to be sung at banquets. It was considered an important social grace to be able to sing *skolia* appropriately, but the guests at this banquet are so forgiving as to overlook an erroneous choice.

1306 *while Spartans under Leonidas fought on land*: The Spartan Ambassador sings of the simultaneous battles of Artemisium and Thermopylae in 480 B.C.E. during the Second Persian Invasion. In the naval battle of Artemisium, the Greek fleet, led by the Athenians, defeated the "Medes" (Persians), while Leonidas famously died fighting to defend the pass of Thermopylae along with three hundred other Spartans.

1346 *Athena a' the Brazen House*: "Athena of the Brazen House" is the citadel-goddess for the Spartans, as Athena Polias is for the Athenians.

1349 *the Eurotas*: The Eurotas is the main river of Laconia. Starting near the border of Laconia and Arcadia, it flows south for fifty-one miles and empties into the Laconian Gulf.

1358 *Leda's daughter*: Leda's daughter is Helen of Troy. We should think, here, not of the adulterous wife of Menelaus but rather of the maiden-goddess of Spartan cult who was the patron deity of adolescent females.

ABOUT THE NORTON LIBRARY

Exciting texts you can't get anywhere else

The Norton Library is the only series that offers an inexpensive, student-friendly edition of Emily Wilson's groundbreaking version of Homer's *Odyssey*, or Carole Satyamurti's thrilling, prize-winning rendition of the *Mahabharata*, or Michael Palma's virtuoso terza rima translation of Dante's *Inferno*—to name just three of its unique offerings. Distinctive translations like these that are exclusive to the Norton Library are the cornerstone of the list, but even texts originally written in English offer unique distinctions. Where else, for instance, will you find an edition of John Stuart Mill's *Utilitarianism* edited and introduced by Peter Singer? Only in the Norton Library.

The Norton touch

For more than 75 years, W. W. Norton has published texts that are edited with the needs of students in mind. Volumes in the Norton Library all offer editorial features that help students read with more understanding and pleasure—to encounter the world of the work on its own terms, but also to have a trusted travel guide navigate them through that world's unfamiliar territory.

Easy to afford, a pleasure to own

Volumes in the Norton Library are inexpensive—among the most affordable texts available—but they are designed and produced with great care to be easy on the eyes, comfortable in the hand, and a pleasure to read and re-read over a lifetime.

W. W. NORTON & COMPANY
Independent Publishers Since 1923